Praise for *Inside the Minds*

"This series provides a practical and focused discussion of the leading issues in law today." – John V. Biernacki, Partner, Jones Day

"*Inside the Minds* draws from the collective experience of the best professionals. The books are informative from an academic, and, more importantly, practical perspective. I highly recommend them." – Keith M. Aurzada, Partner, Bryan Cave LLP

"Aspatore's *Inside the Minds* series provides practical, cutting edge advice from those with insight into the real world challenges that confront businesses in the global economy." – Michael Bednarek, Partner, Shearman & Sterling LLP

"What to read when you want to be in the know—topical, current, practical, and useful information on areas of the law that everyone is talking about." – Erika L. Morabito, Partner, Patton Boggs LLP

"Some of the best insight around from sources in the know" – Donald R. Kirk, Shareholder, Fowler White Boggs PA

"The *Inside the Minds* series provides a unique window into the strategic thinking of key players in business and law." – John M. Sylvester, Partner, K&L Gates LLP

"Comprehensive analysis and strategies you won't find anywhere else." – Stephen C. Stapleton, Of Counsel, Dykema Gossett PLLC

"The *Inside the Minds* series is a real hands-on, practical resource for cutting edge issues." – Trey Monsour, Partner, Haynes and Boone LLP

"A tremendous resource, amalgamating commentary from leading professionals that is presented in a concise, easy to read format." – Alan H. Aronson, Shareholder, Akerman Senterfitt

"Unique and invaluable opportunity to gain insight into the minds of experienced professionals." – Jura C. Zibas, Partner, Lewis Brisbois Bisgaard & Smith LLP

"A refreshing collection of strategic insights, not dreary commonplaces, from some of the best of the profession." – Roger J. Magnuson, Partner, Dorsey & Whitney LLP

"Provides valuable insights by experienced practitioners into practical and theoretical developments in today's ever-changing legal world." – Elizabeth Gray, Partner, Willkie, Farr & Gallagher LLP

"This series provides invaluable insight into the practical experiences of lawyers in the trenches." – Thomas H. Christopher, Partner, Kilpatrick Stockton LLP

ASPATORE

Aspatore Books, a Thomson Reuters business, exclusively publishes C-Level executives and partners from the world's most respected companies and law firms. Each publication provides professionals of all levels with proven business and legal intelligence from industry insiders—direct and unfiltered insight from those who know it best. Aspatore Books is committed to publishing an innovative line of business and legal titles that lay forth principles and offer insights that can have a direct financial impact on the reader's business objectives.

Each chapter in the *Inside the Minds* series offers thought leadership and expert analysis on an industry, profession, or topic, providing a future-oriented perspective and proven strategies for success. Each author has been selected based on their experience and C-Level standing within the business and legal communities. *Inside the Minds* was conceived to give a first-hand look into the leading minds of top business executives and lawyers worldwide, presenting an unprecedented collection of views on various industries and professions.

INSIDE THE MINDS

Navigating Adoption and Surrogacy Laws

Leading Lawyers on Recent Trends and
Best Practices for Nontraditional
Family-Building Cases

ASPATORE

Contents

Understanding the Complexities Involved in Adoption and Surrogacy Cases

Katherine A. Harmon

Partner

Mallor Grodner LLP

ASPATORE

Introduction

My firm practices in the areas of matrimonial law, business law, and estate planning, primarily for high net worth individuals. We handle all types of cases in these areas, including divorces, custody disputes, child support, paternity, grandparent visitation, children in need of services, and of course, adoption and surrogacy.

I started handling adoption cases by representing parents in stepparent adoptions. I enjoy this area of family law because at the end of the day you are helping create a new family instead of dividing a family that already exists. In this chapter, I hope to touch on the different types of surrogacy agreements and adoptions and also the potential pitfalls of each.

Types of Surrogacy Laws

Surrogacy law has evolved as medical advancements have evolved. Now, it is possible to have a surrogate carrying a child that is not biologically related to them (gestational surrogacy) whereas there was a time when most surrogates were likely impregnated using their own egg through artificial insemination (traditional surrogacy).

If the surrogate is a traditional surrogate—where they are providing the egg— then they will be the biological parent of the child that is born. In some states that do not enforce surrogacy contracts, if the surrogate decides they do not wish to proceed with the surrogacy agreement, then the law would consider them as the parent to the child and could place the child with them under the theory that biological parents have superior rights to adoptive parents.

Most states are cautious about allowing a surrogate to be paid for serving as a surrogate versus simply being reimbursed for expenses and paid a stipend of sorts for carrying the child to term. The concern is that we do not wish to "buy a baby" from anyone and instead want to ensure that the expenses being paid are reasonable. That does not mean that a surrogate cannot be reimbursed for "donating" eggs to a couple or that they cannot receive remuneration for the surrogacy; it simply means that the court will look carefully into any agreement that seems to be providing payment for the child instead of reimbursing the surrogate for her expenses and also providing her with a stipend of sorts during the pregnancy.

Surrogacy laws vary widely by states, but fall into the following categories:

1. Criminal penalties for entering into a surrogacy contract
2. Surrogacy contracts void and unenforceable but still occur
3. Permitted in a manner defined by case law or statute
4. Permitted because there is no case law or statute either allowing or not allowing

Criminal penalties for entering into a surrogacy contract. In these states, merely entering into a surrogacy contract could result in criminal penalties for both the surrogate and the potential parents. In these states, it would be highly unlikely that you would find an attorney willing to draft a surrogacy agreement for fear they were participating in an illegal endeavor.

Surrogacy contracts void and unenforceable but still occur. This is where Indiana's laws are currently. In states where this is the case, parties can and do enter into surrogacy agreements. However, both parties to the contract have to be counseled that, should there be any dispute, the agreement cannot be enforced in a court of law. In these states, it is particularly important to inform the potential parents as to the pitfalls of entering into these types of agreements because, should the surrogate change their mind and wish to withdraw from the contract, there are no means by which the contract can be enforced. These states also make it much more difficult to simply have the potential parents' names placed on the birth certificate at birth and often require a subsequent adoption proceeding to occur.

Permitted in a manner defined by case law or statute. In these states, there are laws that exist and define each party's rights and obligations under the surrogacy agreement. In these states, it is much easier to craft an enforceable surrogacy agreement because each party knows what they are required to do and, if there are disputes, they can be enforced in a court of law. These states may allow the potential parents' names to be placed on the birth certificate at birth, thus negating the need for a subsequent adoption.

Permitted because there is no case law or statute allowing or not allowing. These states are akin to the "wild west" in that there are no rules in place and thus no guidance as to what may occur should there be a dispute with the surrogacy agreement. While these states do not forbid surrogacy agreements, they make it much more difficult to draft an agreement that may be enforceable because there are no guidelines in place as to what may or may not be allowed.

General Views of the States

Most states appear to be silent on whether surrogacy will be allowed and have no case law or statutes to provide guidance on how to proceed when seeking a surrogacy agreement. States also vary widely on what they will allow an intended parent to pay for a surrogate. Most will allow for the payment of a fee to the surrogate and the provision of insurance and medical expenses, but will also closely scrutinize as to whether someone is attempting to "buy a baby."

Indiana Policies

I practice in Indiana. In Indiana, surrogacy agreements are void and against public policy.[1] The statute forbids the inclusion of terms in a surrogacy agreement that require the surrogate to provide a gamete to conceive a child, become pregnant herself, or waive her parental rights or duties. *Id.* Since these provisions are key provisions in any surrogacy agreement, we must advise clients entering into surrogacy agreements in Indiana that they run the risk of being unable to enforce the agreement should the surrogate change her mind.

Thus, Indiana by statute does not enforce surrogacy agreements. While they are not illegal *per se* (i.e., no one would be prosecuted for entering into a surrogacy contract), individuals entering into surrogacy agreements here must be informed that should the surrogate not follow through with the agreement, Indiana law would not enforce the agreement.

Traditional Surrogacy

In Indiana, assuming we have a "traditional" surrogacy agreement where the surrogate mother provides the egg and the prospective adoptive father provides the sperm, if the surrogate does not abide by the agreement, then the father can file a petition to establish paternity and seek to have custody of the child. Should that occur, the surrogate could be ordered to

---

[1] Ind. Code Ann. § 31-20-1-1 (West).

pay child support to the father. On the flip side, the father could be required to pay child support to the surrogate. Thus, most individuals in Indiana wishing to enter into a surrogacy agreement will travel to a state that allows surrogacy.

There was a recent case in Indiana where the parties conceived a child by surrogacy but wanted the mother's name to be placed on the birth certificate instead of the surrogate's name without needing to go through the process of doing a formal adoption, so they filed to disestablish maternity. The court ruled that a married woman who acted as a surrogate for another couple cannot petition to disestablish her maternity because it would cause the child to be "declared a child without a mother." The issue arose in *In re Paternity of Infant T.*[2]

In that case, S.T. acted as a surrogate for M.F. She was implanted with an embryo fertilized by M.F.'s sperm and an unknown donor's eggs and became pregnant. M.F.'s wife planned on adopting the child once it was born. M.F., S.T. and S.T.'s husband C.T. jointly filed an agreed petition to establish M.F.'s paternity and disestablish S.T.'s maternity.

The trial court denied the petition and certified it for interlocutory appeal. The court on appeal held that "S.T.'s petition to disestablish maternity is not cognizable. It would not be in the best interests of the child, and would be contrary to public policy, to allow the birth mother to have the child declared a child without a mother. And it would be inconsistent to allow for petitions to disestablish maternity when petitions to disestablish paternity are forbidden."[3]

The court on appeal did reverse the trial court's denial of the petition regarding M.F. and remanded to the trial court to enter an order establishing M.F.'s paternity, because the Indiana Supreme Court has made clear that a joint stipulation between the birth mother and the putative father constitutes sufficient evidence to rebut the presumption that the woman's husband is the father. Here, all the parties stipulated that M.F. is the biological father of the infant. Thus, that was sufficient evidence to rebut the presumption that S.T.'s husband was the father of this child.

---

[2] *In re Paternity of Infant T.*, 991 N.E.2d 596 (Ind. Ct. App. 2013)
[3] *Id.*

However, the court found that their holding does not exclude the indirect disestablishment of maternity, such as in *In re Paternity & Maternity of Infant R.*[4] The indirect disestablishment of maternity requires a putative mother to petition the court for the establishment of maternity and to prove her maternity by clear and convincing evidence, not simply by affidavit or stipulation. If the putative mother satisfies her burden of proof, the establishment of maternity in her would indirectly disestablish maternity in the birth mother.

Given that this case was decided in Indiana, it would only apply to Indiana cases. However, the reasoning behind this case may be cited in other jurisdictions as persuasive authority.

Gestational Surrogacy

Indiana law has not addressed a situation involving a surrogate who wished to keep custody of a child conceived through gestational surrogacy in which the mother and father were the biological parents of the child and the surrogate was merely the carrier. I assume in that case Indiana would allow the biological parents to have custody given the presumption in favor of biological parents.

Same-Sex Couples

Most of our same-sex couples wishing to have a child instead pursue adoption. While Indiana law does not allow for same-sex couples to marry, it does allow them to do a two-parent adoption. If one of the partners is the biological parent of the child, then Indiana will allow the adoption to proceed as akin to a stepparent adoption without terminating the rights of the natural parent. If neither party is the biological parent of the child, then Indiana law will still allow both parties to adopt the child and be listed on the birth certificate.

The laws in other states vary. Some allow a single gay or lesbian parent to adopt; others allow both parties to adopt; and some ban adoption all together for gay or lesbian parents.

---

[4] *In re Paternity & Maternity of Infant R.*, 922 N.E.2d 59 (Ind. Ct. App. 2010).

Special Considerations for Single Parents

In my experience, it is often difficult finding a mother who wishes to place her child with a single parent when there are options available for placement with a couple. Often, single parents seeking to adopt will first serve as foster parents and then pursue adoption through the foster care system; however, some states do not allow single individuals to adopt. The same applies for surrogacy cases involving single parents. Again, it is often difficult finding an individual to serve as a surrogate for a single parent.

I think there often is a bias against single fathers wanting to adopt and many individuals will not consent to an adoption by a single father. Often, those individuals are left to seek adoption by first fostering a child, assuming the state in which they live does not ban single individuals from fostering children. Some states make parties in a surrogacy agreement be married before they can proceed with the surrogacy. Some states not only ban surrogacy for single individuals, but also ban them for gay and lesbian individuals, whether seeking to adopt as a couple or as individuals.

Interestingly enough, if a single father is able to find an individual willing to serve as a surrogate for him, it is an easier process for him to be the biological parent to the child—assuming he is capable of fathering a child— because medically, it is an easier process to do an insemination instead of the transfer required for a gestational surrogate. If a single mother wishes to have a child through a surrogate, assuming she is physically capable of producing a viable egg, she would need to find a surrogate who is willing to serve as the gestational surrogate.

In cases where there is only one parent adopting or seeking a surrogate, it is extremely important to have an estate plan in place that determines what will happen to the child in case of the parent's untimely demise.

Rights of Adoptive versus Biological Parents

In most states, until such time as an adoption is granted or the documents consenting to the adoption are signed, the biological parent has superior rights to the adoptive parent. Adoptive parents seeking to overcome that presumption often face a high burden of showing that the biological parent is unfit or has abandoned the child.

Unless a biological parent is proven to be unfit, most states will require the parent to consent to the adoption. Some states allow for pre-birth consents while others require the consent be signed after birth. Some states make consents that are signed irrevocable without proof of fraud or duress, while others will allow the consent to be withdrawn provided notice is filed within a certain period of time—often up to thirty days after birth. Still, other states will not allow for consent to be withdrawn if the child has been placed with the prospective adoptive parents.

In Indiana, foster parents who have cared for the child do not receive any special consideration under the law. However, if the Child Protective Services case is still open, that division must either consent to the adoption or the adoptive parent must prove the consent is being unreasonably withheld. In my experience, caseworkers are much more willing to consent to the adoption by a foster parent than by another individual, unless the foster parent does not wish to adopt.

The Role of the Attorney

Attorneys need to know if their client is mentally sound enough to pursue an adoption or surrogacy case, knowing that there may be a negative outcome. Attorneys also need to ensure their clients have realistic expectations about the process, what is involved, and the potential pitfalls. Those pitfalls could be the surrogate or biological parent failing to follow through with the process, the child being born with some medical difficulties, or a process that takes longer than expected.

Attorneys also need to ensure their clients are appropriate candidates in that they do not have a criminal record or history with Child Protective Services that could disqualify them from being able to adopt or participate in a surrogacy arrangement.

Adoption Cases

In adoption cases, attorneys get involved at various stages in the process. Sometimes parents will come to us with a child in mind to adopt and then we are involved only in moving the case through the legal process. We can also get involved with helping the prospective adoptive parents find an available child to adopt.

Surrogacy Cases

In surrogacy cases, attorneys also get involved at various stages in the process. We can be consulted prior to the parties trying to find a potential surrogate or after the parties have found a surrogate and are merely trying to reach an agreement as to the terms of the surrogacy agreement prior to the pregnancy occurring.

In my initial meeting with a client, whether it is for an adoption or a surrogacy agreement, I detail to them the laws in Indiana and what they can expect to encounter as the process unfolds. It is at this initial meeting that I make sure they are aware of the potential pitfalls of the process (i.e., that the birth mother or surrogate could change their mind, etc.) and try to ensure they are ready to take that risk. If I have concerns about whether or not they could handle this process, I will refer them to a mental health professional for evaluation. Given that both adoptions and surrogacy agreements can be quite stressful, it is very important to know going into the process whether or not the individuals who are participating in the process are willing and able to undergo the process.

Best Practices for the Attorney

Given the state of law surrounding surrogacy in Indiana, I often recommend parties seeking to have a child to instead pursue adoption. I first need to determine whether it is extremely important for them to have a child that is related to them biologically—in which case we need to pursue surrogacy—or if they instead just wish to have a child regardless of whether or not the child is biologically related to them.

The parties then need to determine if they wish to pursue domestic or international adoption. While international adoption is often more expensive, it can be a more secure process in that, usually, the child is being adopted from an orphanage where there will be no parent contesting the adoption or having second thoughts and instead the concern will be satisfying any roadblocks set forth by the country from which we are trying to adopt. Many other countries have age limits for adoption or will not allow same-sex couples to adopt. So, for older individuals or same-sex couples, their ability to adopt from a foreign country may be limited. It is important in recommending an international adoption to know where the parties are interested in adopting from and what rules may limit their ability to adopt from that client.

With domestic adoptions, unless the party is pursuing a child from foster care—in which case they would likely need to be certified as a foster parent first—there is always the concern that the birth mother or father will change their mind and terminate the adoption process before it is completed. It is important to ensure the clients know this possibility from the start of the process.

The trend now seems to be moving toward open or semi-open adoptions and away from closed adoptions. When my clients are discussing doing an open or semi-open adoption, I need to ensure they have realistic expectations about what that entails. Are they willing to exchange pictures only or are they willing to allow the biological parent to call and visit the child? If we are doing an adoption where there will be post-adoption contact of any kind, all the parties involved must have a realistic expectation of what is involved, and the attorney must make sure that is resolved prior to the adoption being finalized. Any agreement for post-adoption contact should be in writing so it is clearly understood by all parties.

The "Best Interest of the Child" Standard

The "Best Interest of the Child" standard is an overarching view that indicates the court must consider what is best for the children when determining where they should be placed. In child adoption cases, the court must determine whether it is best for the child to be adopted.

Different states will look at different things when determining what is in the child's best interests. Some of the factors they look at are the child's connection to each parent, the child's age, the child's connection to their family and community, whether there is a history of domestic violence, and the wishes of the child and parent.

In Indiana, the court in an adoption will require the potential adoptive parents to first either obtain the biological parent's consent to the adoption or show their consent is not required. Then they need to show that the adoption is in the child's best interests. If the potential adoptive parent is not able to prove it is in the child's best interests for the adoption to proceed, then the court can deny the adoption petition.

Conclusion

Going forward, I believe the areas of adoption and surrogacy will continue to evolve as the medical advancements and beliefs of our society continue to evolve. With more states allowing same-sex marriages to occur, I see the prohibitions against same-sex adoptions that occur in some states being overturned. I also see more birth mothers or surrogates being more open to allowing same-sex couples to adopt their children.

Although surrogacy is now an easier process than it used to be, due to the costs involved and the potential risks, it seems that people are still more willing to lean toward adoption versus surrogacy. It also seems like more birth mothers are looking for open adoptions instead of the traditional adoptions where there was no contact once the child was placed with the potential adoptive parents.

For a period of time, it appeared as if the wave of the future was going the route of international adoption. However, given the issues that have occurred in some foreign adoptions and the fact that some states have banned citizens from the United States of adopting children in those countries, it appears as if more people are now returning to domestic adoptions.

Some potential parents and attorneys are not cognizant enough of the feelings of the birth mother or surrogate, and thus there are misunderstandings and hurt feelings that arise and complicate the process unnecessarily. It is key that all parties entering into these types of agreements have realistic expectations and are clear as to both their expectations and feelings as the process unfolds. Thus, any issues can be addressed before they snowball into much bigger problems.

My advice for attorneys who practice in these areas is to be sensitive to the needs of their clients and also be sure to inform them of the potential pitfalls of the endeavor they are about to undertake.

Potential for Future Change

The biggest change in this area of law will be related to any advances in medicine that create additional surrogacy options. I also think there will be an impact from the change in mindset related to gay and lesbian couples and their ability to adopt or obtain a child through surrogacy. I would anticipate that, as laws advance and allow same-sex couples to marry, they may also expand their rights to adopt or obtain a child by surrogacy in states that do not currently allow this to occur. Also, if same-sex marriage is recognized by a state, then the concern about a single person being able to adopt would be alleviated, because it would be a situation where the parties were married.

Attorneys need to be sure to keep abreast of changes in law and also to attend any legal education classes that are offered about the changes in law.

To ensure I am aware as to the changes in laws that are occurring in these areas, it is important to look for classes being taught in states other than Indiana so I am aware of the arguments that are being made in those states, both for and against adoption and surrogacy agreements, so I can be better prepared to argue for an expansion of the law in Indiana. Ideally, it is important to take these classes on at least a yearly basis if they are offered.

Advice for Being a Successful Attorney

The key to being a successful family law attorney is being able to communicate with people on a level that they are capable of understanding. It is also extremely important to understand that our clients are coming to us often during the worst times of their lives—e.g., the end of their marriage, the possible loss of their children or money, etc.—and being able to empathize with them and ensure that they feel their concerns are being adequately addressed. It is also key that their concerns are handled on a timely basis. Failing to respond for a period of time can make them feel as if they are being ignored.

Often, individuals coming to see us have some mental health issues or are in need of counseling, treatment for substance abuse, or other potential issues. It is important to have a team of counselors and other experts that you can work with to address those concerns. I have several counselors I refer to frequently that are familiar with the issues that arise in the family law setting and can address them.

These skills are developed best by practicing them over the years and implementing them in day-to-day communications with clients. Also, it is important to ask the clients what they need from you and make sure that they know up front what help you can and cannot offer.

Key Takeaways

- In surrogacy cases, courts will look into any agreement that seems to be providing payment for a child instead of simply reimbursing the surrogate and providing a small stipend during the pregnancy. This is done to ensure that no one is simply just trying to buy a baby.

- In some states, including Indiana, it is important that individuals entering into a surrogacy agreement understand that the laws of those states will not enforce the agreement should the surrogate not follow through.

- When working on a case where there is only a single parent seeking adoption or a surrogate, it is important for that individual to have an estate plan in place stating what should happen to the child in case anything should happen to that individual.

- If considering adoption it could be beneficial to start as foster parents. While foster parents do not receive any special consideration under the law, if the CPS case is still open thus requiring consent from the caseworker for the adoption, the caseworker is much more likely to consent to the adoption by the foster parent(s) than another individual(s).

- Ensure your clients have realistic expectations about the processes involved with surrogacy or adoption. They must understand what is involved and the potential pitfalls or complications they could encounter.

Katherine A. Harmon, partner with the firm of Mallor Grodner LLP, is a certified family law specialist, as certified by the Family Law Certification Board of the Indiana State Bar Association. She was named a Super Lawyers® Rising Star, in 2010, 2011, 2012, and 2013. Ms. Harmon is a member of the Indiana Trial Lawyers Association and the Indianapolis Bar Association. She serves as a volunteer attorney with the Marion County Court Pro Bono Project and the Protective Order Pro Bono Project. Ms. Harmon also serves as a volunteer guardian ad litem, ensuring children have legal representation in contentious court cases.

Ms. Harmon has extensive experience representing clients at both the state and appellate court levels in all aspects of family law, including adoptions (child and adult), child support establishment and arrearages, cohabitation agreements, custody proceedings, divorce and legal separation, domestic partnership agreements, grandparent custody and visitation, guardianships, jurisdictional matters involving child support, custody, and parenting time, modification proceedings (custody, parenting time and child support), paternity actions, prenuptial agreements, postnuptial agreements, and protective orders.

Ms. Harmon believes the key to successful representation of her clients is her ability to have the knowledge and preparation necessary to aggressively represent clients in court while also having the ability to problem solve and reach creative solutions to avoid the necessity of a hearing if possible.

Dedication: To my brother Chris; to Aunt Betty, for inspiring me to enter the practice of law; to my parents David and Jean for convincing me that I can do anything I set my mind to; to my husband Patrick for his constant source of love and support; and to our unborn son, who is already my greatest accomplishment in life.

Traps for the Unwary: Ethical Considerations

Karen K. Greenberg

Partner

Konowitz & Greenberg

ASPATORE

Introduction

Law is my second career. I was an elementary school teacher and after eight years, I decided to go to law school. The primary reason for going to law school was to get pregnant. I had been married for those eight years, and was having difficulty getting pregnant. This was the decade of the 1970s and the best the medical field had to offer was the fertility drug clomid, also known as clomiphene, or the old adage, just forget about it and you will find yourself pregnant. Doctors told me to shake up my life; immerse myself in a distraction. So, law school it was. I graduated, *cum laude*, but childless.

I then began to research adoption and am proud to say, my research, no pun intended, proved fruitful. I successfully adopted two children as infants and found myself with a fifteen-year-old, who came and never left. My three children, now all adults, taught me more than law school ever did. And, it was my experience in building my family, and its path, that led me to learn more about family building and the law.

There was another reason I went to law school. My brother, Steven, my law partner for more than twenty-five years, made me go; or rather, the people who sat next to him in the Boston Garden, during those glorious Celtic days of Larry Bird and Robert Parrish, playing against the likes of Julius Irving, Randy Smith, and Bob McAdoo, did. For the entire first half of one such game, my brother unrelentingly urged me to go to law school. As soon as the whistle blew signifying the end of the first half, the people in the adjacent seats, who also held season tickets, blurted out: "For God's sake, Karen, tell him you'll go to law school so we can enjoy the rest of the game!"

Our law firm, Konowitz & Greenberg, began with Steven's first office, in the attic of our parents' home. We have continued to evolve. Steven's practice focuses on mergers, acquisitions (not dissimilar to adoption and assisted reproductive), and corporate law—representing mom and pops to national and international corporations and commercial law.

My practice focuses on Family Law. The umbrella of Family Law encompasses creating families through adoption and assisted reproduction. Some people, including attorneys, are cavalier enough to call this "Happy Law." These two areas may be the most heart-wrenching practices in the law. Understanding the complexities of these two avenues to family building is critical to achieving the desired outcomes.

In my years of practicing law, I have had the opportune experience to serve in a variety of roles as an attorney in family building. Initially, I represented agencies. Massachusetts is an agency state, which requires adoptive placements be overseen by a Massachusetts licensed adoption agency, unless the petitioner is a blood relative of the child sought to be adopted, or the petitioner is a stepparent of the child sought to be adopted or the petitioner was nominated in the will of the deceased natural parent[1] of the child as a guardian or an adoptive parent.[2]

As I continued to grow in my practice, I received calls from other agencies requesting I represent parents contemplating an adoption plan. In accordance with the Code of Massachusetts Regulations[3] there is certain information that the adoption agency, also known as the licensee, must provide in writing at the time of intake. Among the information is a statement that the birth parent(s) have the right to their own attorney, and that the licensee's attorney does not represent the birth parent(s).[4] It was when I began to represent expectant parents, and those who had given birth, in advising them of their rights, that I learned how and why adoption does not lead to everyone popping champagne corks. The more I practiced adoption law, the more I realized the challenges that accompany a plan to adopt, and determining whether to make an adoption plan.

As assisted reproductive technology continued to become a likely alternative for many seeking to build a family, and those who wanted to assist in that family building, I began to realize how similar the pitfalls in adoption are to those in assisted reproductive technology. As a result, my practice focuses primarily on bringing an end to the hemorrhaging in each field. The purpose of this chapter is to spotlight the roots of plans that go awry.

A sure factor that leads to discord and often the unraveling of the most well-laid plan rests with the attorney. In particular, it is when the attorney

---

[1] As an aside, I have often wondered what is meant by "a natural parent."
[2] Mass. Gen. Laws Ann. ch. 210 §2A (West).
[3] 102 Mass. Code Regs. § 5.09 (2013).
[4] 102 Mass. Code Regs. § 5.09(1)(f).

takes on more than one role in the case, representing the interests of more than one party. The attorney does an injustice to the client and the client is at a disadvantage, vying for the attorney's focus and allegiance. Other times, the attorney fails to delineate her role in the matter and a party, to his detriment, misunderstands the attorney's responsibilities. There are other times when the attorney blatantly represents more than one party in the matter, which lays the groundwork for unexpected havoc to break out.

This chapter highlights some of the challenges in both adoption law and assisted reproductive technology.

Basically Speaking

I have endeavored to walk in the shoes of some of my clients, finding many of the labels and choice of words used in creating families, frankly speaking: archaic, misunderstood, and downright insulting. I have clarified terms for some often intertwined words that can result in misunderstanding legal consequences. I have taken the liberty to modify the language to make up for past disparaging intimations that reflect stale and disrespectful notions. Moreover, many of the terms are illogical. For the purposes of this chapter, please note the following:

Birth Parents

There is no such thing as a birth mother until after the mother who gave birth to the child makes an adoption plan and the plan is in place. Similarly, there is no such thing as a birth father. And, as of this writing, I know of no father who has ever given birth.

Give the Baby up for Adoption

Remember the phrase, "up with which I will not put"? I will never forget it. Picture this, recently retired first and second grade teacher, first day of first year property class, the professor, Judge Cornelius J. Moynihan,[5] referring to

---

[5] Judge Moynihan, former justice of the Superior Court of Massachusetts, professor at Boston College Law School and Suffolk University Law School, authored PRELIMINARY SURVEY OF THE LAW OF REAL PROPERTY (West 1940) *and* INTRODUCTION TO THE LAW OF REAL PROPERTY: AN HISTORICAL BACKGROUND OF THE COMMON LAW OF REAL PROPERTY AND ITS MODERN APPLICATION (West 1962). Judge Cornelius J. Moynihan was also

Winston Churchill, called out a student's name who promptly replied, "Up with which I will not put." I felt doomed. No one ever gives a child "up."

Giving up is when one secedes from something. No one can secede from a child, try as he or she might! In an ideal world, parent(s) who make an adoption plan for their child do so because it is in the best interests of the parent(s) and the child. Equating an adoption plan with giving up a child is rude and ignores what should be the true spirit of making an adoption plan.

Out of Wedlock

A child cannot possibly be born out of wedlock, because the child cannot be considered "in wedlock" and is generally not married when born, or when an adoption plan is being considered. Rather, a child may be born of two parents who are not married to each other.

Biological Mother/Genetic Mother

A biological mother/genetic mother is a woman who contributes her egg to produce the resulting child, whom she intends to parent.

Biological Father/Genetic Father

A biological father/genetic father is a man who contributes his sperm to produce the resulting child, whom he intends to parent.

Intended Parents

Intended parents are individuals who intend to become the legal parents of the child produced as a result of a gestational or surrogacy agreement.

Gestational Carrier

A gestational carrier is a woman who carries a developing fetus in her uterus until it is born. The developing fetus is not the egg of the gestational carrier.

---

known for committing the alleged Boston Strangler convicted on armed robbery and morals charges on Jan. 18, 1967 to Walpole for life, revoking the previous order which had suspended execution of a life sentence to Walpole after Albert Desalvo escaped the previous day from Bridgewater State Hospital.

Gestational Surrogacy

Gestational surrogacy refers to a contractual situation whereby a woman
agrees to have an in vitro fertilized embryo implanted into her uterus, and
then agrees to carry the resulting child to term. She further agrees to
relinquish her parental rights upon the birth of the child. The implanted
embryo is often, but not always, produced by the gametes (egg and sperm)
of the intended parent(s).

Surrogate

A surrogate is a woman whose egg assisted in creating the embryo she is
carrying. The surrogate is biologically related to the embryo.[6]

Traditional Surrogacy

Traditional surrogacy refers to a contractual situation whereby a woman
agrees to become impregnated, typically by artificial insemination using her
own egg and the sperm of another man. The sperm is usually from the
intended father of the resulting baby. She agrees to carry the resulting child
to term and thereafter relinquish her parental rights to the child. She is
considered the biological, genetic, and gestational mother of the resulting
child because the surrogate uses her own egg.

Who is a Mother? Who is a Father?

It is difficult to define mother and/or father because state laws regarding a
mother and a father vary. In some states, a woman who gives birth to a
child is considered the mother for all intents and purposes. Other states
recognize gestational carrier agreements and make a distinction, often
referring to the mother as the intended mother, and the father as the
intended father. Similar to other terminology in the emerging practice of
assisted reproductive technology, certain words have varying meanings and
the tried and true dictionaries, as well as statutory definitions, have yet to
keep up with areas of law that continue to evolve. For example, there are
variations on the definition of a mother:

---

[6] There are still some schools of thought who do not use the term biologically *unrelated*
because the Gestational Carrier's biological "material" is intertwined with the
implantation and growth of the embryo.

As to adoption absent abandonment the mother is known. That is generally a certainty, unless she was a party to a gestational contract. I had a case in which the gestational carrier fled to a surrogacy unfriendly state to ensure she would be recognized as the mother.

The *Merriam-Webster Dictionary* states the full definition of MOTHER is "to give birth to; to give rise to; produce; to care for or protect like a mother."[7] The Law Dictionary states a mother is a woman who has borne a child; a female parent; correlative to "son" or "daughter." The term may also include a woman who is pregnant.[8] The traditional definition of mother remains in states that prohibit surrogacy agreements. For example, Michigan prohibits all surrogacy agreements, regardless of sexual orientation of the individuals involved.[9]

And, there is the range of who is, and who may be the father:

- The biological father, determined by DNA testing;
- The legal father, who either

  o Was married to the mother at the time of conception; or
  o Signed acknowledgment of parentage under the pains/penalties:

    ▪ Caused his name to be/or placed his name, on the birth certificate;
    ▪ Because he *wanted* his name on the birth certificate;

- The putative father, as named by the mother;
- The putative father as named by the mother, tracked down by the state taxing authorities because mother receives state assistance to support their child; and
- The unknown, unnamed putative father.

---

[7] Merriam-Webster Dictionary, Mother, *available at* http://www.merriam-webster.com/dictionary/mother.

[8] *See Howard v. People*, 185 Ill. 552, 57 N. E. 441 (1900); *Latshaw v. State ex rel. Latshaw*, 156 Ind. 194, 59 N.E. 471 (1901). *See also* LawDictionary, Mother, *available at* http://thelawdictionary.org/mother/.

[9] Mich. Comp. Laws Ann. §§ 722.851-861 (West 2009); *Doe v. Attorney Gen.*, 487 N.W.2d 484 (1992); *Doe v. Kelley*, 307 N.W.2d 438 (1981); *Syrkowski v. Appleyard*, 362 N.W.2d 211 (1985).

Massachusetts has one lone statute that is the closest the legislature has come to legislating assisted reproductive issues and defining a mother and a father. The child born to a married woman and her husband is the legitimate child of the mother and her husband when a married woman gives birth to a child conceived through artificial insemination with the consent of her husband.[10]

On the other hand, Illinois has a comprehensive statute that came into effect in 2005, known as the Gestational Surrogacy Act.[11] The Gestational Surrogacy Act clearly delineates its purpose; definitions; relevant language; the rights of parentage; eligibility; requirements for a gestational surrogacy contract; the duty to support; and the establishment of the parent-child relationship.

Comparing Massachusetts' lack of statutory requirements and definitions with the Illinois statute only underscores the need for more comprehensive statutory law to clarify terms to avoid misunderstandings and unethical tactics.

The Uniform Parentage Act

The Uniform Parentage Act (UPA), amended in 2002, provides clear definitions for the rights, or lack thereof, for donors, husbands and intended parents.

For example, a donor is not a parent of a child conceived by means of assisted reproductive.[12] The court may authorize the use of gestational carrier agreements so long as certain conditions are met.[13] These conditions include the gestational carrier agrees to the pregnancy by means of assisted reproductive technology, and if married, her husband relinquishes all parental rights to the child and the intended parents become the parents of the child.[14] However, the agreement is only valid after a court issues an order which, *inter alia*, validates the gestational agreement and declares that the intended parents will be the parents of a child born during the term of the agreement.[15]

---

[10] Mass. Gen. Laws Ann. ch.46 § 4B (West).
[11] 750 ILCS 47/1 *et seq.* (2005).
[12] UNIF. PARENTAGE ACT § 701.
[13] UNIF. PARENTAGE ACT § 801.
[14] UNIF. PARENTAGE ACT § 801(a).
[15] UNIF. PARENTAGE ACT § 803(a).

Taxable Income or Not???

State laws vary as to whether a carrier may be compensated, and if compensated, whether the money is taxable income. A dispute as to whether the compensation received for being a carrier, or donating eggs or sperm, is taxable is currently before the US Tax Court. As of this writing, the US Tax Court has been asked to determine whether the $20,000 the donor received for her eggs is a matter of a contract or tort law.[16] The IRS is arguing the money is compensation for the eggs, while the donor claims the compensation should be likened to an award for pain and suffering.[17] The ruling may also impact people who donate sperm and blood plasma.[18]

Understanding the various terms and catchphrases ensures that all parties recognize the implications to, and the responsibilities and rights of each other. All of the participants expect, *or should expect*, proper guidance. The attorney should be exceedingly familiar with the protocol in his/her state. If the case also involves out-of-state parties, the fast lane to a malpractice case is the failure to consult an attorney of the other state(s) who is known to have a good reputation[19] as a practitioner in those areas of family building. Gaining a perception of that state's do's and don'ts will enable the practitioner to map out a game plan to which the client may refer.

It is all too simple for an attorney to practice law without a license when drafting and reviewing a contract to be enforced under the laws of a state in which she/he is not authorized to practice. Contracts are often riddled with terms and language that are against public policy and cannot and will not possibly be enforced. An excellent and common example is referencing the conditions that mandate whether or not the carrier may abort the fetus. Another example is dictating each minutia the carrier may put in her mouth, her daily routine and habits. Contracts should distinguish when money given to the carrier is reimbursement for expenses, or income for services rendered; nonetheless, tax law and not the language of the contract will apply. It is critical to know whether state law prohibits compensation and

---

[16] *Id.*
[17] *Id.*
[18] *Id.*
[19] The American Academy of Assisted Reproduction Attorneys lists its members on its website: www.aaarta.org.

under what circumstances a 1099 must issue.[20] Consultation with an accountant or tax attorney as to any tax implications is wise and hopefully will avoid the words that hurt every attorney's ears: "You never told me."

Traps for the Unwary

Adoption law and assisted reproductive technology law are not static; rather the laws and practices continue to evolve as we learn from our mistakes and society or the courts demand more. Unlike contracts or torts, which have basic principles grounded in the case law and statutes, family building law continues to establish and amend basic principles. I have yet to hear the words "black letter law" applied to either practice.

Uniform Laws

The Uniform Parentage Act has not been enacted in all states. Lawyers must rely upon state law in such circumstances.[21]

State Law

State laws often lack clear distinctions between Surrogacy Agreements and Gestational Agreements. In the first instance, the egg of the surrogate is used; in the second instance, the egg may be either from a donor or the intended mother. Currently, states vary on whether any contracts to give birth to a child for another are valid. Some states prohibit such contracts altogether, while others prohibit only those that involve compensation. Some states allow for gestational carrier contracts, but do not recognize traditional surrogacy contracts, and again, may vary on the legality of compensation terms.

---

[20] Lawfuel Editors, *IRS in Dispute Over Fertility Payment*, LAWFUEL, (Mar. 2, 2014), *available at* http://www.lawfuel.com/irs-dispute-fertility-treatment-payment/.

[21] The Uniform Parentage Act (UPA) is a set of uniform rules for establishing parentage, which may be adopted by state legislatures on a state by state basis. It declares equal rights for children regardless of their parents' marital status. Originally approved by the National Conference of Commissioners of Uniform State Laws (NCCUSL) in 1973, its current revision combines the UPA, the UPUFA (1989, with revisions), and the Uniform Status of Children of Assisted Conception Act (1989, with revisions) into a single act. It includes nine sections on genetic testing. *See* http://definitions.uslegal.com/u/uniform-parentage-act/.

Naturally, states, and often countries, absent statutory or case law, vary in the procedures for the birth certificate to issue with the intended parents named as the legal parents. Some states allow for pre-birth orders; others require the child be born and proof of birth and proof of the origin of the egg and or sperm. And again, there are states that clearly prohibit such arrangements, and the only means to secure the birth certificate is by adoption.

Case Law

Much case law has developed as a result of poorly drafted state statutes, the lack of state statutes, and of course, parties creating their agreement as they see fit, rather than in accordance with public policy and constitutional considerations.

A major concern still exists with surrogacy agreements. A glaring example is that the person who gives birth to the child is the mother of the child, regardless of the terms of the contract, unless there is law within that state to the contrary.

Traditional Surrogacy

In a recent case out of Wisconsin, the Wisconsin Supreme Court[22] upheld a Parentage Agreement for traditional surrogacy and adoption of the child. The Court stated the Parentage Agreement to be valid unless enforcement was contrary to the best interests of the child.[23]

In that case, the surrogate carrier became pregnant through artificial insemination using her egg and the intended father's sperm. The surrogate had been best friends with the intended mother since childhood. Regardless of their long-established bond, the surrogate was unwilling to terminate her parental rights. As can happen in such cases, contract or no contract, the intended mother had no rights, and there was no statutory scheme to support the intended mother's position.[24]

The Court did not view the entire contract as enforceable, specifically the requirement that the surrogate terminate her parental rights. However, the

---

[22] *In re F.T.R.*, 2013 WI 66, 349 Wis. 2d 84 (2013).
[23] *Id.*
[24] *Id.*

Court did accept severing the termination of parental rights portion of the contract, and then enforcing the provisions regarding custody and placement.[25]

As to the public policy issue, the Court took the position that a contract may be void on public policy issues, but only if it determines, after weighing the interests, that the interests in enforcing the contract clearly outweigh the interests in upholding the policy the contract violates. The case was remanded for a determination of custody and placement.[26] The case attained the desired outcome in enforcing the intentions of the contract. Nevertheless, the means was at tremendous cost, financially, emotionally, and psychologically.

Same-Sex Couples

Same-sex couples must be cognizant that if one partner gives birth, the other partner has no legal relationship unless the child is adopted. The exception, of course, is if the partners are recognized under state law as married. Nevertheless, I continue to urge my clients to adopt the child, ensuring that both parents' parental rights have been established even though Massachusetts recognizes same-sex marriages.

For example, in *Della Corte v. Ramirez*,[27] same-sex married partners are each the legal parent of a child conceived by artificial insemination born during the marriage. As a result, joint legal custody may be granted in a divorce and the same principles in determining the best interests of the child will also apply.

In *Hunter v. Rose*,[28] the Massachusetts court recognized a child conceived by artificial insemination to a California registered same-sex domestic partnership as the child born to a marriage. Both women are legal parents and the court has the discretion to grant primary custody to the most-fit parent.[29]

And yet, please keep in mind, as noted in *A.H. v. M.P.*[30] a child was conceived by artificial insemination by donor sperm to a woman in a same-

[25] *Id.*
[26] *Id.*
[27] *Della Corte v. Ramirez*, 81 Mass. Ap. Ct. 906, 961 N.E.2d 601 (2012).
[28] *Hunter v. Rose*, 463 Mass. 488, 975 N.E.2d 857 (2012).
[29] *Id.*
[30] *A.H. v. M.P.*, 447 Mass. 828, 857 N.E.2d 1061 (2006).

sex relationship. The former partner, who was neither the biological nor the adoptive parent of a child, claimed to be a *de facto* parent but was denied custody and support rights.[31] The court determined the relationship between the former partner and the child did not rise to the level of a parent because she was not the child's primary caretaker and had other interests above that of the child.[32]

Had the partner adopted the child, the former partner would not have to go through the exercise of establishing herself as a parent. Given the facts of the case, the former partner may have had a better chance of achieving her goals if she had adopted the child at the outset. At this stage, it was too late, because consent of the former partner would be required.

In *T.F. v. B.L.*,[33] a same-sex couple agreed to have a baby. One partner was artificially inseminated. Post birth, mother sought child support from her now former partner. The court rejected the idea of "parenthood by contract" and ruled their agreement to co-parent unenforceable as against public policy.[34] Nothing in the record showed a distinct consideration in return for child support apart from the core, unenforceable promise to co-parent. The court refused to create a child support obligation on the mere promise to co-parent.[35] Again, had the partners adopted the child, the burden of custody and a parenting plan would not have been as great.

Adopting Internationally—The Hague

The Hague Convention on the Protection of Children and Co-operation in Respect of Inter-Country Adoption (Hague) is an international agreement to safeguard inter-country adoptions. The Convention, enacted May 29, 1993, establishes international standards of practices for inter-country adoptions. The United States signed the Convention in 1994, and the Convention entered into force for the United States in April 2008.[36]

---

[31] *Id.*
[32] *Id.*
[33] *T.F. v. B.L.*, 442 Mass. 522, 813 N.E. 2d 1244 (2004).
[34] *Id.*
[35] *Id.*
[36] *See* Hague Conference on Private International Law, *Convention of 29 May 1993 on Protection of Children and Co-operation in Respect of Intercountry Adoption, available at* http://www.hcch.net/index_en.php?act=conventions.text&cid=69.

The Hague applies to all adoptions between the United States and the other counties that have joined it, called Convention Countries. According to The Hague, those who adopt through a Convention Country receive greater protections.[37]

There are several aspects to The Hague that are traps for the unwary. Among them are that a child may be adopted only after it is first determined that the child is eligible for adoption in accordance with the laws of the child's country of birth. Efforts must support that there is no suitable home and permanent placement for the child in the child's birth country.[38]

Therefore, if there is an aunt or uncle in the United States who wants to adopt his/her niece or nephew living in the child's native country, even though the child is living in dire poverty with his/her family, it cannot be done, unless the child's two living parents, who were the last legal custodians, signed an irrevocable consent to adoption, and were determined to be incapable of providing proper care for the child.[39]

Another key issue is that only adoption service providers, individuals, and licensed agencies evaluated and approved by one of the Department of State's designated Accrediting Entities may offer adoption services with Convention Countries. In many instances, the person(s) seeking to adopt from a Convention Country may be working with an agency to conduct the home study and post-placement supervision *and* accredited agency adoption service providers, individuals, and licensed agencies to secure the adoption.

---

[37] As of this writing, I am in the process of winding down and resolving an international adoption with a Convention Country. Based upon the facts of the case and the documented medical and psychological conditions of the siblings, the Hague offered no protection as to the siblings' circumstances and the prospective adoptive mother's understanding of the children's background. This adoption was not in the best interests of one of the siblings, and technically that sibling was not eligible for adoption, but was able to come to the United States on the "coattails" of the younger sibling. A member of that country's Central Authority was sent to discuss the case with my client and me after the court issued a preliminary injunction, preventing the removal of the child from her home. As a result of the case, I am told that as a result of this case, that particular country is reexamining its policies and the Hague accredited agencies with whom they work.

[38] Dep't of State, Intercountry Adoption, *Who Can Be Adopted*, (updated Oct. 2013), available at http://adoption.state.gov/adoption_process/how_to_adopt/childeligibility.php.

[39] Dep't of State, Intercountry Adoption, *Intercountry Adoption from A to Z*, *available at* http://adoption.state.gov/content/pdf/Intercountry_Adoption_From_A_Z.pdf.

Up to Date Information About a Country

It is critical to know about the country from where the clients intend to adopt. A country's adoption history and policies are valuable information to know before committing to a particular agency that has a program with the country. An excellent source is the US State Department's Bureau of Consular Affairs' webpage that lists country information.[40] The Country Information section describes whether a country is party to The Hague Adoption Convention, provides names and contact information of a country's adoption authority, and describes the eligibility requirements for prospective adoptive parents and for children to be adopted. In addition, the Country Information offers contact information, in addition to the role of the court and adoption agencies, as well as adoption statistics. And, most importantly, the website keeps updating country specific adoption alerts and notices regarding the adoption process in a particular country.[41]

For example, by going on the site, one can learn up-to-date relevant adoption information, such as:

- On February 6, 2014, India, though its Central Adoption Resource Authority (CARA), announced the partial lifting of the suspension for children classified by CARA as special needs.[42] CARA informed the US Central Authority that, effective February 3, 2014, Indian passport holders may register to adopt Indian children not classified as special needs.

- On February 4, 2014, Kenya formed a new adoption committee, and is now processing adoptions. Prior to that time, on January 7, 2014, the Kenya Adoption Committee had been disbanded.[43]

Another good example is that on January 16, 2014, Haiti ratified The Hague Adoption Convention. Technically, Haiti is ready to submit to become a Hague country in accordance with the requirements of the Convention. The

---

[40]Dep't of State, Intercountry Adoption, *Country Information*, *available at* http://adoption.state.gov/country_information.php.
[41] *Id.*
[42] *Id.*
[43] *Id.*

Convention on Protection of Children and Co-operation in Respect of Inter-Country Adoption will enter into force for Haiti on April 1, 2014. There will be a determination made as to whether Haiti has met the requirements of the Convention and the Inter-country Adoption Act of 2000 with respect to individual adoption cases by the date that the Convention enters into force for Haiti. This site will also be used to confirm when the Department of State will be able to certify Convention adoptions from Haiti.[44] Additional information provides whether and how adoptions will be processed prior to the United States' certification of Convention Adoptions from Haiti.[45]

Regrettably, there is no guarantee, no matter where the potential adoptive parent(s) may be in the international adoption process, that it will be completed. International countries do not always have stable governments and adoption laws could change overnight. An unfortunate example is Russia. On December 28, 2012, President Vladimir Putin signed into law Russian Federal Law No. 186614-6, which prohibits the adoption of Russian children by US citizens.[46] This law went into effect on January 1, 2013. The law bans adoption of Russian children by US citizens, bars adoption service providers from assisting US citizens to adopt Russian children, and requires termination of the US-Russia Adoption Agreement.[47]

Sadly, there were and still are many families caught in this change of the law. On December 28, 2012, the law was signed, effective January 1, 2013, three days later. It was not until January 22, 2014 that the Russian government finally allowed those children whose adoptions had court approval prior to January 2, 2013 to be given to their parents.[48]

Visas

A word of caution to all: Children, who enter the United States on an I-4 visa, come into the United States under a guardian petition to be adopted in

---

[44] Dep't of State, Intercountry Adoption, *Country Information supra* n. 40.
[45] *Id.*
[46] Sobranie Zakonodatel'stva Rossiiskoi Federatsii [SZ RF] [Russian Federation Collection of Legislation] 2012, No. 186614-6.
[47] Dep't of State, Intercountry Adoption, *Country Information supra* n. 40.
[48] *Id.*

the United States.[49] These children are issued a green card and do not automatically acquire US citizenship. The children are lawful permanent residents until the adoption is full and final. Once finalized, parents file a form with United States Citizen's and Immigration Service (USCIS).[50] USCIS will issue a Certificate of Citizenship if the child meets the requirements for automatic citizenship.[51]

Most international adoptions are finalized in the child's country of origin. In those circumstances the child enters the United States with an I-3 visa. If entering with an I-3 visa, there is nothing further to do to secure citizenship for the child.[52] The child becomes a United States citizen by operation of law.[53]

Nevertheless, finalizing the adoption in accordance with the laws of the child's state is still recommended for several reasons. Many governments are not stable, and the child's country of origin could decree all previous adoptions in that country void. Circumstances may arise that could lead to a determination by the USCIS that the adoption in the child's country was void *ab initio*. By finalizing the adoption in the United States the child's adoption is fully recognized by the USCIS. It is a relatively simple procedure.

Several years ago, I represented a young woman who had been adopted by her uncle, in her native country, in accordance with the laws of her country. She entered the United States with her uncle, and applied for and received a green card. A few years later, when she applied for citizenship, USCIS deemed her adoption void, because the adoption decree from her country of origin lacked a signature, which USCIS determined vital. The issue was whether the laws of her native country required that particular signature at the time of her adoption. Her uncle had relied upon the validity of the adoption in their country of origin and although they had petitioned the Probate and Family Court in their jurisdiction to adopt, in accordance with the laws of the state in which they lived, the petition was not filed until two weeks after her sixteenth birthday.

---

[49] Dep't of State, Intercountry Adoption, *U.S. Visa For Your Child, available at* adoption. state.gov/us_visa_for_your_child.

[50] *See* Form N-600.

[51] U.S. Dep't of Homeland Security, U.S. Citizenship and Immigration Services, *After Your Child Enters the United States, available at* http://www.uscis.gov/adoption/ bringing-your-internationally-adopted-child-united-states/after-your-child-enters-united-states.

[52] Child's Citizenship Act of 2000, Pub. L. No. 106-395, 114 Stat. 1631 (Oct. 30, 2000).

[53] *Id.*

USCIS threatened to revoke her visa. Luckily, her immigration attorney was able to secure several continuances while he researched the requirements at the time of her adoption. I was able to petition the court for her adoption decree be entered *nunc pro tunc* to a few days before her sixteenth birthday.

One other important factor—the court will retain all of the documents necessary for the adoption, albeit copies. However, the documents are on file with the court and will remain there.

<u>Assisted Reproductive Technology Internationally</u>

Many people looking to build their families through assisted reproductive technology seek out carriers in other countries, primarily because costs are less. One must be cognizant of any assisted reproductive laws and immigration laws of the country. Immigration laws have not kept pace with the assisted reproductive technologies, which result in bringing a child born as a result of assisted reproductive technology from the country in which he/she was born by the intended parents into the United States.

The Immigration and Nationality Act (INA) Sections 301 and/or 309 govern the United States citizenship at birth to a child born abroad. A United States citizen parent must have a biological connection to the child to transmit United States citizenship.[54] If a child is conceived through assisted reproductive technology, the father must be a United States citizen and the genetic parent of the child. The mother must be a United States citizen and the genetic mother of the child or the carrier and the legal mother at the time and place the child is born.[55] It is the United States Department of State that determines whether the child is eligible for citizenship, even if the law of the country allows for gestational carrier agreements and recognizes the intended parents as the legal parents.[56]

---

[54] The Immigration and Nationality Act of 1965 (INA), Pub. L. No. 89-236, §§ 301-09, 79 Stat. 911 (Jun. 30, 1968).

[55] U.S. Dept. of State, *Important Information for U.S. Citizens Considering the Use of Assisted Reproductive Technology (ART) Abroad, available at* http://travel.state.gov/content/travel/english/legal-considerations/us-citizenship-laws-policies/assisted-reproductive-technology.html.

[56] *Id.*

Because this determination is done on a case-by-case basis, the best determination is by DNA evidence. Of course this cannot be done until the child is born. And, unfortunately, one has to consider that a mistake can be made by the clinic in any of the procedures.[57] It is critical for United States intended parents considering an international gestational carrier arrangement to consult with an immigration attorney, particularly when one of the parents is not going to be genetically related to the child, to ensure entry into the United States. Oftentimes the child will not be recognized as a citizen of the country in which he/she is born, irrespective of the United States requirements.[58]

A United States citizen parent who has a biological child in an international country, even if by a non-United States citizen surrogate, may find relief by applying for a Consular Report of Birth Abroad of an American Citizen (CRBA) and a US passport for the child at the US Embassy or Consulate in the country where the child was born.[59] The CRBA does certify that the child born abroad is a United States citizen, and does not determine the legal parents of the child. If, under local law, the second parent is able to demonstrate a legal parental relationship with the child, that parent may be listed on the CRBA. But the CRBA is not determinative of the second parent's status.[60]

Obtaining a Passport for the Child

There is also the issue of obtaining a United States passport for the child. Here, again, the parents may have to provide medical and documentary evidence of the child's conception and birth and such other evidence as would demonstrate the biological connection between the child and the parent. Of course, DNA testing would be the best evidence.

Ethical Considerations

Adoption law and assisted reproductive technology are fraught with ethical considerations. Two key issues for attorneys are contracts and conflicts in representation.

---

[57] *See, e.g.* Kristine S Knaplund, *Baby Without A Country: Determining Citizenship for Assisted Reproduction Children Born Overseas*, U. DENV. L. REV. (forthcoming 2013).
[58] *Id.*
[59] *See* U.S. Dept. of State, *Important Information for U.S. Citizens Considering the Use of Assisted Reproductive Technology (ART) Abroad supra* n. 55.
[60] *Id.*

Contracts

Drafting gestational carrier contracts are jam packed with traps for the unwary and ethical considerations. The first problem that comes to mind is the drafter. Many times the intended parents are in one state and the gestational carrier is in another. The contract may be drafted in accordance with the laws of the intended parents' state (State A). The contract could also be drafted in accordance with the state with a more favorable law because enforceability of gestational carrier contracts vary from state to state (State B). The carrier's attorney may be from the carrier's state (State C).

Simply put, the attorney from State C should not advise his/her client as to the laws of State B, unless also admitted to practice in State B. Following that reasoning, the intended parents may be represented by an attorney in State A and their attorney should not advise them as to the laws of State B. And yet, it does happen. There are legal and ethical pitfalls that include, but are not limited to, practicing law without a license, enforceability of the contract, and procedures particular to the jurisdiction.

Varying Laws State to State

The scarcity of statutory authority in some states may cause a quagmire, as can statutes that have gestational and surrogacy laws. For example, the Illinois statute, known as the Gestational Surrogacy Act,[61] lacks guidelines on some of the thorniest contract provisions.[62] Ms. Ross discusses a host of problematic issues, which, quite frankly, underscore the consequences of not only bad drafting, but also the violation of public policies. Contracts often push the boundaries close to, if not blatantly, unconscionable. Note some of the following examples:

The gestational carrier's medical autonomy may be compromised by terms in the contract that allow the intended parents to make medical decisions regarding the fetus, the food ingested by the carrier, as well as invasive procedures and aborting if the fetus is found to have developmental concerns.

---

[61] 750 ILCS 47/1 *et seq.*

[62] *See, e.g.* Heather Ross, *Gestational Surrogacy in Illinois: Contracting the Unknown,* 26 DCBA BRIEF 16 (Dec. 2013).

I found myself representing a family who wanted to adopt the expected child of a gestational carrier. The intended parents were insisting the carrier undergo an abortion. The carrier refused and fled to an unfriendly gestational carrier state. The intended parents claimed that the carrier was in breach, and repudiated all financial obligations under the contract. The gestational carrier claimed the intended parents were in breach when they denied her any further financial support. Clearly, this was not something contracted for by any of the parties.

The gestational carrier knew that she could not be forced to abort the fetus. However, the gestational carrier was extremely concerned as to what would happen to the child upon birth and sought out a family willing to adopt and properly care for the anticipated child.

Nevertheless, state laws vary as to whether protecting fetal life may take priority over the mother's or carrier's right to medical autonomy.[63]

Conflicts of Interest

Code of Ethics

Problematic are state codes and bar association codes of ethics that define standards for a conflict of interest and a protocol that allows for dual or even multiple representation. For example, the American Bar Association,[64] the American Academy of Adoption Attorneys (AAAA (pronounced Quad A)),[65] and the American Academy of Assisted Reproductive Technology Attorneys (AAARTA)[66] each have their own Code of Ethics.

Massachusetts's Conflict of Interest[67] prohibits the representation of a client if the representation of that client will be directly adverse to another client,

---

[63] *See, e.g. Id.*
[64] MODEL RULES OF PROF'L CONDUCT R. 1.7.
[65] AAAA, established in 1990, is a not for profit fellowship of attorneys, judges, and law professors throughout the United States and Canada. Admission is determined by attaining a certain level accomplishment in the law regarding adoption law.
[66] AAARTA, established in May 2009, is a credentialed, professional, not for profit fellowship of attorneys, judges and law professors throughout the United States and Canada. Admission is determined by attaining a certain level accomplishment in the law regarding assisted reproductive technology.
[67] RULE 3:07. MASS. RULES OF PRO'L CONDUCT AND COMMENTS R. 1.7(a)(1) & (2).

unless the lawyer reasonably believes the representation will not adversely affect the relationship with the other client and each client consults after representation. The caveat here is that both parties must consent.

AAAA promulgated a Code of Ethics that, similarly to the Massachusetts Rules of Professional Conduct, allows for multiple representations, with written full disclosure and consent.[68] AAARTA promulgated a Code of Ethics that, similarly to the Massachusetts Rules of Professional Conduct, allows for multiple representations, with written full disclosure and consent.[69]

Each of the Code of Ethics mentioned above prohibit multiple representations, and yet all have escape clauses, which allow for multiple representations. With due deference to my AAAA and AAARTA colleagues, the ethical codes are not sufficient. Full disclosure and written consent are not always adequate and many of the participants may still find themselves at a disadvantage.

The Role of the Attorney

Call me old-fashioned but I can only represent one interest at a time. This may seem rather logical, but is not always the case in both adoption matters and assisted reproductive technology. My years of experience as an agency attorney taught me well of the conflicting interests in adoption. Many attorneys who practice adoption law and/or assisted reproductive technology represent more than one party purposely, or fail to distinguish their specific roles in the matter. By doing so, the attorney should have his/her malpractice insurance carrier on speed dial.

Agency Attorney

For example, at the time of engagement with an adoption agency, the prospective adopting client may not know or understand that the dual representation will adversely affect the relationship. The agency attorney's interests should be aligned with the agency only and the agency's sense of duty for several reasons.

---

[68] American Academy of Adoption Attorneys, Directory 2013-2014 (2013).
[69] American Academy of Assisted Reproduction Attorneys, Directory 2013-2014 (2013).

The agency attorney may have drafted the contracts the prospective adopting parent(s) will be required to sign. Regardless of the drafter, these contracts have specific clauses that favor the agency and are not negotiable. The clauses limit the agency's liability, requiring the agency be held harmless and indemnified. The contract may also have a clause that requires the prospective adopting parent(s) to pay all legal expenses, should litigation ensue, even if there was no indication at the time of placement that there would be such risk.

The agency contract generally controls whether the child will be placed for adoption with the client, for numerous reasons. As an example, the placement may be high risk because one or both of the parents' rights have not been terminated and litigation may ensue. The child may have been born with severe developmental issues and the placement may not be appropriate for the child, or perhaps, the prospective parent(s).

More fundamentally, it is the agency that will conduct the home study to determine whether the client will qualify to become an adoptive parent. This is a subjective standard, and in the past, agencies have been sued for failure to approve a home study on the grounds that the denial of an approved home study was not reasonable.[70]

A significant example is when a parent who has placed a child comes forward and wants to challenge the placement. Examples are the mother wanting to revoke her surrender, or the father refusing to consent to his rights being terminated and to the adoption. This, again, is an area laden with conflicts. Ethical rules may not and cannot address some of these situations. It is the agency's role and obligation to ensure the parent receives counseling prior to making a decision whether to parent or not. If the parent determines she wants to parent, the agency has lost that placement and there is an economic impact. The corollary is that it is preferable for a parent to contemplate the process and come to a decision to parent, rather than have the parent relinquish his/her rights and regret it soon after.

A more difficult situation is when the father refuses to give his consent. Then, what position does the agency take? The agency should take the

---

[70] Examples of denial included concerns about the applicant's physical or mental health, existence of criminal background, or former drug or alcohol addiction. Each of these concerns may have varying degrees of gravity.

position as to what is in the best interests of the child only. Rather than proceed with the placement, the agency ought to turn to the father, understand his plan for the child, and determine whether or not the father is fit to parent and if his plan is in the best interests of the child. Sadly, oftentimes the agency is too quick to side with the prospective adoptive parent as a knee-jerk reaction.

I was recently involved in a disrupted adoption, precipitated by the prospective adoptive father being arrested by the FBI for viewing child pornography. The Interstate Compact on the Placement of Children[71] revoked their permission for the child to be in Massachusetts, and ordered the child be returned immediately to the sending state. The child was then placed in a new pre-adoptive home. The Massachusetts agency immediately took the position that the child should not have been removed from the Massachusetts family, despite the arrest of the pre-adoptive father on a major matter which cuts right to the safety and best interests of the child. I suspect the position was grounded in the desires of the Massachusetts family, and not the child's well-being.

The same principles relevant to the contracts holds true for attorneys who represent the assisted reproductive center (Center) and the intended parent(s). The goals of the Center and the intended parents may not be the same, and, under certain circumstances, collide.

Trends

Assisted reproductive technology continues to make new law. As the case law keeps on growing, states without comprehensive statutes will enact them. Just as the secrecy of adoption has diminished, and structured laws have given way to openness, I anticipate the same path in assisted reproductive technology.

The value of having a comprehensive health and psychosocial history of the birth parent(s) is equally true in assisted reproductive technology. The healing aspects of learning more about one's family of origin and perhaps meeting them, in due course, will spill over into assisted reproductive technology.

---

[71] Association of Administrators of the Interstate Compact on the Placement of Children, *Interstate Compact on the Placement of Children*, www.aphsa.org/content/ AAICPC/ en/home.html.

In my practice, I have worked with donors and intended parents and carriers who want to establish and maintain a relationship. However, I am still weighing whether or not these arrangements should be formalized and enforceable, and let me tell you why.

In Massachusetts, formalizing post-adoption contact grew out of cases with the Department of Children and Families, where children were taken out of their homes because of abuse and/or neglect. Quite often it was found to be in the best interests of the child to have ongoing contact with his family of origin, when reunification was no longer an option. This approach made sense particularly in those cases where the child had lived with the parent(s), had a relationship with the parent(s), and emotionally and psychologically it was the sound thing to do. Initially the arrangement for contact was incorporated into the judge's order, based upon the circumstances of the case. Regrettably, this approach became a convenient way to influence a birth parent to voluntarily have her parental rights terminated. Continuing contact is not suitable in all adoptions.

Eventually, Massachusetts enacted statutes that gave continuing contact agreements (Post-Adoption Contact Agreement/Agreement). As long as the Agreement strictly complies with the language in the statute, the court has the ability to enforce the agreement.[72] One of the key features in the statute is that the court does not have the power to increase birth parents' rights beyond the terms of the contract. The court only has the ability to strictly enforce the Post-Adoption Contract or reduce or terminate the birth parents' contact with the child.[73]

Several years ago, I represented an adoptive family challenging a Post-Adoption Contact Agreement, seeking to void the agreement in its entirety. The case was emotionally grueling on each of the parties to the contract. The court vitiated the Post-Adoption Contact Agreement and reduced quarterly weekend visits in the adoptive family's home to two yearly three-hour visits supervised by an adoption social worker in a visitation center. My clients had adopted two other children and had successful open adoption agreements with the birth families, to the extent that eventually no one bothered to follow the terms of the agreement. A

---

[72] Mass. Gen. Laws Ann. ch. 210 § 6C (West).
[73] Mass. Gen. Laws Ann. ch. 210 § 6D.

Post-Adoption Contact Agreement is not a cure-all, and cannot be entered into when the parties are unable to respect boundaries.

Applying the concept of enforceable Post-Adoption Contact Agreements to assisted reproductive technology situations is laden with landmines. Cousins may be genetic siblings, aunts, genetic mothers and uncles, genetic fathers. Having a full understanding of the importance of boundaries *and* respecting those boundaries can be a difficult if not impossible challenge. When the situation goes sour, so does everybody.

Tidbits of Advice

How to Avoid Becoming Unwary?

Do your due diligence. Research, research and research again. Consult other attorneys in the field. Develop a network of attorneys, statewide and nationally who practice in these areas. Attend seminars, statewide and nationally. Adoption law and assisted reproductive law know no boundaries. Pick up the telephone, call the State Department and the relevant state court, and continue to associate with attorneys who practice law in creating families.

Listen to Your Gut

Adoption law and reproductive technology law are unique in that each area of the law focuses on creating a family. Poor judgment, hasty strategies, and lack of knowledge can prove devastating and costly, financially and emotionally. We are advising our clients about being responsible for another life, and/or creating a family for someone else. As my brother Steven says, take your time, focus, but make sure you have a good time!

Manage Your Client's Expectations

It is critical in any area of the law to make sure your client's expectations are within the realm of attainability, substantively and financially. Although I may have a discussion with my clients about a certain aspect of their case, or an overview of the process, there are times when I do not think a discussion will suffice. I often follow up with a letter memorializing our discussion and request the client to contact me if I have misconstrued anything.

Prepare and Send Your Client a Game Plan Letter

Initially, when I take on a case, I do a letter we refer to as our "Game Plan Letter." The Game Plan Letter is specifically tailored to each client's needs, concerns, and specific issues in his/her matter.

The Game Plan Letter will include:

- A detailed outline of the theory of your case
- A step-by-step plan of all of the action steps expected to be taken
- An explanation of the procedural rules, the requirements of the procedural rules, how they relate to the specific case and why
- A review of the controlling statutes and pertinent case law
- Precise attention to and an explanation as to why certain aspects of the case may prove more difficult than others, premised upon the facts and circumstances presented

Expect the Unexpected

The client and the attorney must be prepared to expect the unexpected. In adoption law, the mother may decide she wants to parent her baby or an initially unknown, unnamed father may come forward and prove to be the biological father, and he wants to parent the child.

With international adoptions, the child promised may not be the child presented to the prospective adopting family. The child may have hepatitis and not be allowed to enter the United States, and therefore not adoptable by your clients.

In assisted reproductive technology, if working with a surrogate, she may decide to parent the child. In the process of egg removal, the donor may not have kept to the timing schedule and the eggs are not considered of "high quality."

Conclusion

I had several goals in writing this chapter. The first goal was to highlight areas I find to be problematic and challenging. The stale language that continues to be used does not reflect what the experts—be they lawyers, social workers, psychologists, and medical doctors—have come to learn about adoption and reproductive technology. Language is powerful, demoralizing, and easily misconstrued. Language can also be used to de-escalate many of the emotionally charged components.

My second goal was to draw attention to the lack of consistency in the assisted reproductive technology laws. The same is true in the notice provisions in adoption law. For many years Congress has ignored the need for a Responsible National Father Registry that would allow those who may have fathered a child with a woman to whom they are not married, the opportunity to register and receive notice of any potential adoption or guardianship, without depending upon the mother to identify him.

My third goal was to raise issues with which I have been struggling or troubled. I still do not understand how one attorney can represent more than one party in either an adoption or assisted reproductive matter. What particularly concerns me is how the owners of the gestational carrier/surrogacy center can represent the center and the intended parents.

And I also wanted to pass on some tidbits. Turning to trusted advisors, learning to trust my inner voice, road mapping the case for my clients, and going back to the "drawing board" when necessary have served me well.

One of the things I love about our law is that our law keeps evolving and the evolutions reflect our mores. The question remains, however, what came first, the law or the mores?

Key Takeaways

- Notice to Putative Fathers by Publication. If notice by publication is required, and the putative father is unknown, unnamed or of parts unknown, be sure the child's last name includes the mother's last name. Oftentimes the mother's last name may not be recognizable to the interested person.
- Solidifying the Parental Rights of Same-Sex Couples. Even in states where the marriage of same-sex couples is recognized or valid, whether the child was adopted by only one partner, or born by one

partner, both parties must adopt the child to ensure both parent's names are on the birth certificate. This will avoid any challenges to one of the parent's relationship with the child, and allow the court to adjudicate child-related issues if and when necessary.

- International Adoption. It is vital to educate your client as to anticipated circumstances. The child's medical and social-psycho histories may be sparse, the child originally designated may no longer be available for adoption, the child may have health/emotional issues not revealed or known at the time, and once home, there will be a period of adjustment.

- Know whether the country in which your client seeks to adopt is a Hague Country, and if so, that you understand the requirements to adopt a child from a Hague Country, and the agency with whom you client is working is an approved agency. And of course, be sure you are knowledgeable about all aspects of The Hague Convention with regard to international adoption. A critical aspect overlooked by many practicing attorneys is that unless the standard of there being no relatives and/or a suitable placement for the child their client wants to adopt in the child's birth country is met, the child will not be available for adoption.

- Inconsistency in Assisted Reproductive Technology Laws. Some states have no statutory law addressing assisted reproductive technology, only case law, while others have statutes and some states rely upon both. Be familiar with the law of the other state and rely upon an attorney of that state to assist you in your understanding of that state's law. Be on guard for possible breaches of your client's medical autonomy and unconscionable terms to the gestational or surrogacy agreement, and avoid dual representations.

- Above all else, do not lose sight of who you are representing!

Karen K. Greenberg, a partner at Konowitz & Greenberg, Wellesley Hills, MA, practices with her brother, Steven S. Konowitz. As her brother would say, Ms. Greenberg grew up in Newton, MA and Mr. Konowitz grew up in Brighton, MA. Brighton is a neighborhood of Boston, and Newton is an adjacent city, but quite different communities. At the time they lived in Brighton, Brighton was generally a working-class neighborhood, made up of multi-family homes, apartment buildings, and a few single homes. Newton was and still is more of an "upper middle class" city. The reason for the move: schooling for Ms. Greenberg. Mr. Konowitz was a student at Boston Latin School. Boston Latin School, originally an all male school, is a public exam school founded on April 23, 1635. It is both the first public school and oldest existing school in the United States. Ms. Greenberg was not the Girls' Latin School type.

In her first life, Ms. Greenberg, a graduate of Boston University, SED, taught elementary school in Quincy, MA. At BU, she was educated to teach in a multi-level open classroom, on an individualized basis. As the educational pendulum swung back, soon after graduation from Wheelock College, M.Ed., Ms. Greenberg entered Suffolk Law School, graduating cum laude in 1983.

Ms. Greenberg joined her brother while in law school, excelling in photocopying and getting the mail out on time. This was perfect for Mr. Konowitz who continuously prodded her to consult her law professors on a variety of "stumpers." A founding member of the American Academy of Adoption Attorneys, after serving on the Board of the American Academy of Adoption Attorneys, Ms. Greenberg was elected president from 2008 to 2009.

In her thirty years as an attorney, Ms. Greenberg has also developed a domestic relations practice where she focuses on complex, contested, high-conflict family law matters, including divorce, custody, post-divorce, and paternity issues.

Dedication: *This chapter is based upon my collective experience in practicing family building law. I want to acknowledge my children Jed, JennaRose, and Melissa, who, because they dallied before coming into my life, caused me to take an unexpected spin. I want to thank my brother Steven, who is also my partner, for being first and foremost my brother, and yes my biggest and my most critical fan. I want to thank the TEAM at Konowitz & Greenberg, Attorney Arlene Kasarjian, Paralegal Michael Leary, Officer Manager Kristin Cappello, and our latest player, Bernard Posner, for humoring me every day at the office and of course for invaluable support. As I have always said, one is only as good as one's TEAM. I owe tremendous gratitude to the fellows of the American Academy of Adoption Attorneys and American Academy of Assisted Reproductive Technology Attorneys for their brilliance, willingness to share, persistence, and dedication in making vital inroads in two of the most complicated and vulnerable areas of the law. Thank you all.*

Key Elements of Working on Adoption/Surrogacy Cases: Insights for Family Law Attorneys

Brian W. King

Senior Partner

King Crotts Duncan & Jaynes

ASPATORE

Introduction

Being a family lawyer for fifteen years, and a family law specialist for the past six, has led me through an incredible journey of fascinating stories, incredibly resilient people, and a large dose of reality. Oftentimes the legal backdrop takes a backseat to the tapestry of lives that intersect in this area of the practice of law.

I am able to work in the beautiful mountains of North Carolina, and roam courthouses located in areas ranging from small South Carolina towns to Charlotte and other larger municipalities. I enjoy a working relationship with diverse attorneys in both states, who work in a large range of practice areas.

It is my desire that this chapter provide some very specific insight into the actual practice involved in the areas of adoptions and surrogacy.

I find that adoptions are the most rewarding part of any family law practice. No one celebrates losing half of their possessions to a spouse they no longer have, and certainly no one celebrates a custody schedule and dividing the time children spend between homes. However, in adoption cases, the family lawyer is able to permanently change lives, and by definition move the child into a better situation.

There are many legal tightrope issues involved in adoption, however. Many times it is frustrating to consider the amount of time and effort that is being expended during the adoption process—time and money that could be better spent on the adopted child. However, anyone who participates in this area of practice, or has been through an adoption that failed to be completed, can understand why certain safeguards are needed.

The Adoption Client

There is no doubt that the nature of the word "family" is changing. The same can certainly be said about the adoption client. Adoption clients come in many forms. Sometimes they take the form of a young mother who has struggled to raise a child without the benefit of a father for many years. This young mother has now found someone who has stepped into the role of a father to that child, and wants to formalize the situation that is already all but a reality to that child.

Other times, a couple comes into my office, having identified a mother who is having a child they wish to adopt. Sometimes that child has been made known to them through a group or organization; other times a friend has connected the parties. Increasingly, the potential client is a grandparent who has raised their grandchild for so long that adoption seems the most prudent next step.

In yet another example, a young lady once came to me who had literally had a child left on her doorstep. We identified the mother as someone who had met my client at church one Sunday, and thought that my client and her husband would be good parents for a child she had no idea how to raise.

The common factor that is often shared by all of these potential clients is their sheer lack of knowledge with respect to how the adoption process will take place. They are all so concerned about achieving the final goal of bringing a child into their home that they often overlook basic and necessary information about the adoption process.

The Initial Client Interview

I love hearing the stories of my clients. I like to let them talk for about fifteen minutes or so without interrupting them or telling them what I believe is relevant. I think that it is vital to simply listen to what they feel is important about their situation.

A few of my clients tell their story in chronological order, and most of them at least try to do so. I typically take a legal pad, turn it sideways, and draw a timeline across the top while they talk. I let them see me take notes. It encourages them to organize their story without me interrupting their flow. However, most people like to tell stories in a way that highlights important events or people (regardless of the timeline). For example, clients in an adoption often want to jump ahead to the care they will provide for a child. While important, it is much more legally significant for me to understand the nature of the mother giving up the child for adoption. Once, I patiently waited for over a half hour before the client even began talking about the mother. It is important to build the trust with the client, but information needs to be obtained. Therefore, I always divide the bottom of my timeline into three equal boxes, illustrated below.

The first box at the bottom of the timeline is my attempt to draw as detailed a family tree as possible. I have found over time that just because my client refers to someone as an "aunt" does not mean that they are, in fact, an aunt. They may be talking about a cousin, friend, or just someone in the community.

The middle box contains the "facts" that do not fit neatly on the timeline— i.e., a note such as, "Uncle Joe is a registered sex offender," or "the father lives in Austin."

The final box contains the client's "wants." As I listen to the potential client, I believe that it is important that I understand what they "want." Sometimes the potential client has said that they want an adoption, but during the interview it becomes clear that they simply want custody of the child.

TIMELINE ->		
FAMILY TREE:	FACTS:	WANTS:
•	•	•
•	•	•
•	•	•

I try to keep my notes restricted to the original first page of my chart. Especially in the adoption arena, the client is going to fill out many documents with extensive information. There is no need to spend precious amounts of face time (and expensive billing time) attempting to write down every address they mention, or similar information. This task will be performed later on by a paralegal with a lower billing rate, after we have money in our trust account.

When the original ten to fifteen-minute discussion is over, I immediately turn to my computer and begin putting information into our client file. We have been paperless at my office since 2006, and we use software to answer a series of questions in all family law cases. My paper notes will be scanned in after the meeting and shredded. For adoptions, these questions may include:

1. Names and addresses of all relevant parties
2. Name of child and relationship to the adopting parent
3. Where is the other parent
4. Circumstances surrounding the birth of child
5. Date of birth of child (or anticipated birth date)
6. Place of birth, if known
7. Any support from other parent
8. Any contact between child and parent
9. Any prior court order involving custody, support, and/or visitation of child
10. Why should the parent no longer be the child's parent?
11. Length of time they have known the child/parent
12. Nature of relationship
13. Common interests with the child
14. Closeness of the bond all parties have with child
15. Length of time adopting parents have been married, known each other
16. Has there ever been a separation?
17. Do the client(s) understand that if they divorce, possible consequences and responsibilities (child support, custody, etc…)?
18. Do the clients understand that any legal or financial obligation to support or care for child is gone?
19. Does the child own any personal or real property value?
20. Why is the adoption in the best interests of the child?
21. What will the child's name be?
22. Any criminal or other issues that may be of issue
23. Can the clients financially support the child?
24. Do the clients understand that notwithstanding a will, the child will inherit from them as if the child was their natural child?

I want the client to have a fee contract in place before they leave the office. I do not have a set adoption fee. The following has to be considered in setting a fee:

1. Is a termination of parental rights required?
2. Will this be an interstate (or international) adoption?
3. Is this a stepparent adoption?
4. What is the likelihood the mother will change her mind?
5. Is paternity known?

6. Will the parent(s) stipulate to the adoption?
7. Has the child been born?
8. Is an adoption-placement agency involved?
9. Is a state agency (such as Child Protective Services) involved with the family?
10. Is a home inspection/study required by state law?

Setting Goals

Potential clients have varied levels of understanding of the adoption process. Sometimes they have spent hours working with a social worker on the adoption process. They are well informed as to the end result, and have some kind of realistic understanding of the timeline they are facing during adoption.

Often times, however, they do not understand the steps at all. For many, there is a feeling that an absent father should have no bearing in this process. The logic is simple (and probably makes sense from the client's point of view): if the father has not been a part of the child's life up to this point, then the father should have no say in what is happening now. Little thought is often given to identifying who the father is, much less on how to find him.

It is often hard for me to believe how callous some of my clients seem. I believe that certain clients feel that the adoption process is going to be much like a land transaction. Basically, the attorney will run a "title search" to make sure the right "buyer and seller" are present, sign paperwork, and record the adoption in some imaginary Register of Persons. The concept of adoption is a deeply personal and real experience.

Types of Adoption

One area of law in flux across the states is a process known as an open adoption. An open adoption allows the adopting family and the biological parents to exchange identifying contact information. This exchange allows for the parties to remain in contact with one another after the adoption. State laws do not generally prohibit post-adoption communication between the adoptive parents and the birth parents as this is usually a mutual agreement and the adoptive parents have control over who their adopted child communicates with.[1]

Some states have specific laws that make post-adoption contracts legally enforceable.[2] Over half of the states have some sort of legislation that makes these types of contracts enforceable by law.[3] In these states, post-adoption contact is generally permitted so long as the nature and frequency has been deemed appropriate by the court, the contact remains in the child's best interests, and the contact is designed to protect the safety and welfare of the child.[4] Generally, all parties must have agreed to the terms of the contact in writing prior to the finalization of the adoption.[5] There are various limitations on open adoption agreements. Some states limit their enforceability to stepparents and relatives, some only enforce contracts involving children over the age of two.[6] In a few states, relatives of the child, not just biological parents, may continue to have contact after the adoption is complete.[7] Additionally, there are some states that require mediation before entering into these contracts and some courts will consider the wishes of the child when determining the enforceability of the agreement (the age of the child varies by state).[8]

In North Carolina, open adoptions are allowed so long as there is some sort of agreement between a natural parent and an adoptive parent. However, these contracts are not legally enforceable under the law and cannot be used in an attempt to get either party to consent to an adoption.[9]

Qualifications for Adoption: Key Case Law and Legislation

When "fit" biological parents do not want to relinquish their parental rights, it may be almost impossible to force them to do so. In my primary state of

---

[1] U.S. Dep't of Health & Human Services, Child Welfare Information Gateway, *Postadoption contact agreements between birth and adoptive families*, (2011), *available at* https://www.childwelfare.gov/systemwide/laws_policies/statutes/cooperative.cfm.
[2] *Id.* at 2.
[3] *Id.*
[4] *Id.* at 3.
[5] *Id.* at 4.
[6] *Id.* at 3.
[7] *Id.*
[8] *Id.* at 4.
[9] *Id.* at 5.

practice, North Carolina sets forth that written consent of the parents or guardians is required before custody may be terminated.[10] However, a parent's right to custody and control of their children is not absolute and may be challenged. This is typical across the country.

There have been significant changes in the way North Carolina courts have come to look at the issue of biological parental rights over the past twenty years. All states have had to grapple with the Supreme Court of the United States clarifying constitutional rights to parent a child. The most prominent North Carolina case on this issue is the North Carolina case of *Petersen v. Rogers*.[11] Prior to this case, courts would look to the best interests of the child in making a determination with respect to with whom the child is placed. In *Petersen v. Rogers*, the court stated that the United States Supreme Court noted the "rights to conceive and to raise one's children have been deemed 'essential' . . . 'basic civil rights of man' . . . and 'rights far more precious . . . than property rights.'" In addition, the *Petersen* court noted that the US Supreme Court has held that the "integrity of the family unit" is protected by due process. Given these protections, the US Supreme Court has also stated that as long as a parent is "shown to be fit," the state's interest in caring for children is *de minimis*. North Carolina courts have not traditionally recognized that the rights of a biological parent to the custody, control, and care of their children are supreme to the rights of all other individuals. Prior to *Petersen*, the North Carolina courts had previously used the best interests of the child analysis instead of the parental rights analysis. The parental rights analysis may be set aside if the petitioner is able to demonstrate that the biological parents are unfit. The court in *Petersen* noted "absent a finding that parents (i) are unfit, or (ii) have neglected the welfare of their children, the constitutionally-protected paramount right of parents to custody, care, and control of their children must prevail."[12] Ultimately, parents who have lawful custody of their children and are not placing their children in danger have the right to retain custody of their children above all others.

Another reason for the shift from the best interests of the child analysis to the biological parental rights analysis is a due process argument. In *Price v.*

---

[10] NC Gen. Stat. § 48-2-206 and 2-207.
[11] *Petersen v. Rogers*, 111 N.C. App. 712, 713, 433 S.E.2d 770, 772 (1993).
[12] *Id.* at 403.

Howard, the court noted that the petitioner must overcome the due process argument before the best interests of the child analysis will begin.[13] The *Price* court noted "this decision requires a due process analysis in which the parent's well-established paramount interest in the custody and care of the child is balanced against the state's well-established interest in protecting the welfare of children." This is only applicable when the parentage of the child has been established. The right to the care, custody, and control of children by biological parents is a fundamental right; thus, violation of this right is subjected to a strict scrutiny analysis. However, if the parentage of the child has not been established or has been lost by virtue of the parent's action then the violation of due process analysis is not necessary. In this situation the courts will apply the best interests of the child analysis. This places the burden on the petitioner to show that the biological parents are unfit. Absent reports from physicians, mere speculation will not prevail in these cases, making it difficult for petitioners to gain custody from biological parents. To gain custody of a child from its biological parent there must be a showing of neglect or abuse.

The Adoption Process

The process of adoption may be the simplest part of the adoption procedure. Do not let that fool you, however; there are many landmines in this area.

First, make sure you know that everyone involved in the process is, in fact, English-speaking. Most states have adoption forms written in English and Spanish, but ensuring that all of the parties have an understanding of the term "consent to adopt" is vital in the event the adoption is ever legally questioned. Having forms in the language of the signor can aid in that analysis.

The petition to adopt is the basic document that begins the process. Some states have varying forms based on the type of adoption you are dealing with. In some states, a stepparent can file for adoption with a shortened form.

The petition itself will establish jurisdiction, the parties involved, and the basic information regarding the petitioner and the birth of the child. It will account for any property the child may have, or monies due to the

---

[13] *Price v. Howard*, 346 N.C. 68, 75 (1997).

child. It will make determination of any relationship the child has to the petitioner prior to the adoption taking place.

The age of the child is important as well. States have generally adopted the position that a specific age (perhaps twelve, fourteen, or otherwise) is an appropriate age for a child to be a party to the petition of adoption. In those cases, the child should be served with the petition.

The adoption petition is a sworn document, and failure to provide correct information can be the basis of perjury. Therefore, do not overlook this step. I encourage family law attorneys to actually read the acknowledgement out loud to the petitioner, and have the client affirm the petition in front of a notary. Adoption can have very permanent consequences, and the information your client has provided needs to be the basis of the petition. This is further protection for the practitioner, who does not want to be caught in the middle of an improper adoption (for example, a mother who loses custody in one state is now attempting to create a stepparent adoption in another state—or more precisely, in your office).

In cases where the child is located outside of the state, the states operate through the Interstate Compact on the Placement of Children (ICPC), which has been adopted in some form in every state. This process requires the states to communicate through state level agencies, and then to local units. This can be a time-consuming process, and will almost invariably require the involvement of multiple attorneys' offices. At minimum, this is going to double the documents you have to prepare, and at least triple the amount of agencies and governmental entities you have to work with.

If the child protective services department of the state is involved in your case, they may need to be a party to the action. These organizations almost always have resources on the local or state level to aid in this determination. It is imperative to seek counsel in states outside your own or at least consult with the state equivalency to the Department of Health and Human Services. It is, however, not unusual for this department to have its own internal process for adoptions. I believe that it is vital to maintain a strong working relationship with your local adoption case workers and civil department.

The most difficult documents to obtain during the adoption process include the consent to adoption or relinquishment for adoption. If the mother of the child is a minor, there are more protections for that mother. Usually, there is a period of several days during which the parent can revoke the adoption. There are rarely any documents more devastating that come into our offices than the revocation of an adoption after the child has been placed.

I strongly recommend that you have an attorney represent the mother in cases of adoption. Have that attorney meet with the mother and review her rights. Also, have that attorney sign documentation showing that advice was given and the right to revoke was explained.

There is almost always a state home study requirement in an adoption process. Your client will be subject to a background check, have their home inspected, and have friends and family questioned. This process can be expensive, and the client needs to know of these costs up front.

There is a list of medical questions parents are asked for the child to know of any genetic medical issues they may have in the future.

Ultimately, the decree of adoption is signed by the local judge. We like to have a ceremony of the signing of the decree. This decree is sent to the state's vital records department for issuance of a new birth certificate.

What Requirements Do Prospective Surrogates Have to Meet in the State(s) Where You Practice?

North Carolina does not have a statute that specifically addresses surrogacy or surrogacy contracts. However, North Carolina does have various statutes that deal with adoption and lawful and unlawful payment during the adoption process. These statutes potentially indicate that payment for surrogacy violates North Carolina public policy, though there is no law that specifically prohibits it.

To become a surrogate, one must generally go through medical facilities and surrogacy agencies within the state. These facilities assist prospective surrogate parents and each has their own requirements to become a surrogate. In general, a surrogate must be at least twenty-one years old and have given birth to at least one child. Additional requirements include, but are not limited to, a primary physician evaluation including a complete medical history questionnaire, a psychological evaluation, consultation with an OB/GYN, an infectious disease screening, and legal consultation.

How Has This Law Evolved Over the Past Few Years?

In March of 2009, the North Carolina general assembly proposed legislation that would provide guidelines for establishing surrogacy agreements. The bill was not adopted into law but would have provided specific language that would have made surrogacy agreements undeniably legal and provided basic law for what should be included in a gestational surrogacy arrangement.[14] Further, the legislation would have made compensating the gestational carrier acceptable so long as the price was "reasonable."[15]

Currently, there are North Carolina statutes that apply directly to surrogacy without stating as much. N. C. Gen. Stat § 49A-1 states a child or children born through heterologous artificial insemination are to be considered the same as a naturally conceived legitimate child of the husband and wife requesting, so long as they consented in writing to the use of the technique.[16] Under N. C. Gen. Stat §48-10-103 parents may not make payment contingent upon the adoption or relinquishment of a child.[17] Further, §48-3-608 states that consent to the adoption of a child in utero or any other minor can be revoked within seven days after consent is originally given.[18] Each of these statues indicate that payment for the adoption of a child is illegal and any contract regarding payment for the adoption or relinquishment of a child will be deemed void. Further, that the biological parents have a window of opportunity to change their minds about adoption or relinquishment of a child.[19]

The development of the Uniform Status of Children of Assisted Conception Act (USCACA) could provide North Carolina with much needed framework on this issue.[20] USCACA attempts to provide unified structure for the rights of parents who have children through assisted

---

[14] H.R. 510 (N.C. 2009).
[15] *Id.*
[16] N.C. Gen. Stat. Ann. § 49A-1 (West).
[17] N.C. Gen. Stat. Ann. § 48-10-103 (West).
[18] N.C. Gen. Stat. Ann. § 48-3-608 (West).
[19] LEE'S NORTH CAROLINA FAMILY LAW § 17.101 (LexisNexis 5th ed.).
[20] UNIF. STATUS OF CHILD. OF ASSISTED CONCEPTION ACT (1988).

conception.[21] However, so far only two states have adopted the USCACA. North Carolina has not.[22]

What Requirements Do Prospective Parents Have to Meet in the State(s) Where You Practice Before They Can Enter into a Surrogacy Agreement?

Prospective parents must also undergo a screening process before they are able to seek a surrogate. Because there are no laws governing surrogacy requirements in North Carolina, the requirements vary by medical facility. These requirements are very similar to the ones required by the surrogate mother and generally include a physical exam, mental health exam, background check, and sometimes an in-home assessment.

Success of the adoption process is generally assessed through the benefit to the child. The underlying purpose of Chapter 48, as stated previously, is to ensure the best scenario for the child or children involved and to ensure that the adoptive parents are willing and able to take on the responsibility of becoming parents. The best interests of the child are the number one priority of adoption and success is measured by the benefit and well-being that adoption brings the child.

What Must Attorneys Understand About the Way Courts Process Child Adoption Petitions?

For an adoption to be approved by a court, the adoptive parents must file a request for approval, or adoption petition, and participate in an adoption hearing. Notice requirements vary by state, but generally notice should be given to any person required to consent before the hearing takes place. Those required to consent may include birth parents of the child, an adoption agency, the child if of a certain age, or a child's representative.

Typically, some form of home investigation or adoptive study will be done with respect to the adoptive parents. This process verifies that the parents are fit to raise the child. Often done by a social worker, the investigator will assess the home environment then write up a positive or negative recommendation. Information regarding financial stability, marital stability, lifestyle, other children, career commitments, physical and mental health,

---

[21] *Id.*
[22] *Id.*

and criminal background may be of importance. Not only does this study serve as an investigative tool, it also serves as an educational and informative process for the adoptive parents. Awareness of these issues will aid them in realizing the responsibility that comes with becoming the child's legal guardian.

A typical adoption petition includes: names, ages, and address of adoptive parents; name, age, and legal parental information of the child; any existing relationship between the adoptive parents and the child; the legal reason for termination of parental rights; statement regarding the appropriateness of the adoptive parents; and statement that the adoption is best for the child's well-being. Along with the petition, the birth parents' consent or an order terminating the parents' rights may be filed. A request for an official name change for the child is typically filed at this time as well. If the adoption is found to be in the child's best interest at the hearing, the judge will issue an order, or final decree of adoption, and the process will then be finalized. At that time a decision regarding name change will also be ordered.

The court may appoint an attorney or guardian *ad litem* to represent the child and ensure that the child's best interests continue to be upheld during court proceedings.[23] North Carolina, like many states, provide a free brochure (online and off line) of guardianship law. Guardians may represent those under legal age who are considered "infants," the unborn, or the incompetent. The relationship is typically created through court order and ends once the legal action ends. A guardian *ad litem* is legally responsible for representing the well-being of the child or incompetent person and have great power and responsibility. Their duties may include investigating, attending to a child's emotional needs, monitoring the child's family, and shielding the child from the legal experience. While their work is usually extensive, their position is often voluntary or low paid.

Procedures and necessary documents vary from state to state. In North Carolina, an adoption petition must be filed with the clerk of court and state within thirty days after the child is placed with the adoptive parents or

---

[23] Adoption & Child Welfare LawSite, North Carolina Statute Summary, *Adoption specifically Procedure*, *available at* http://www.adoptionchildwelfarelaw.org/ document_detail.php?id=2138

the state has jurisdiction otherwise.[24] Both parents should indicate whether they have lived in the state of North Carolina for the six months immediately prior to the petition being filed. Essential documents include: a description and estimate of the value of any property the child owns, any necessary affidavit of parentage or consent of relinquishment, a certified copy of any court order terminating parental rights or pleading in a pending custody or visitation matter, copies of any required assessments, documentation of the child's health, educational, social, or genetic history if available, any signed copy of authorization forms allowing the child to come into the state, proof of any agreement to release past-due child support, and any required release of identification forms.[25]

In child adoption and surrogacy cases, it is important to always protect the child and keep his or her best interests in mind. Attorneys should thoroughly understand the process for their practicing state and come prepared with all essential documentation.

Conclusion

Family law can be one of the most stressful and at the same time rewarding practices an attorney may have. These issues do not simply develop over a contract or during work hours. Adoption is no different. However, the reward of helping permanently change the outcome for a child in their life is like little else an attorney may do.

I anticipate many changes in dynamics over the next few years as to surrogacy and adoption. Perhaps a streamlining of the process to make this procedure easier for adopting parents may make sense for legislatures, but it must be carefully crafted as to not exceed the constitutional protections laid forth by the United States Supreme Court.

This practice changes lives like no other, and it is important to avoid the pitfalls that may derail that change. I hope you find this practice area as rewarding as I have.

---

[24] Adoption & Child Welfare LawSite, North Carolina Statute Summary, *Adoption specifically Form and Filing of Petition*, available at http://www.adoptionchild welfarelaw.org/document_detail.php?id=2138.
[25] *Id.*

Key Takeaways

- Let the client talk for about fifteen minutes or so without interrupting them. Take a legal pad and draw a timeline across the top while they talk. Include three boxes: one containing a detailed family tree; the second containing the "facts" that do not fit neatly on the timeline; and a third box containing the client's "wants."

- Set your fee based on various factors—i.e., is a termination of parental rights required? Will this be an interstate (or international) adoption? Inform your client that they will be subject to a background check, have their home inspected, and have friends and family questioned. This process can be expensive, and the client needs to know of these costs up front.

- Note that potential clients have varied levels of understanding of the adoption process. Ensuring that all of the parties have an understanding of the term "consent to adopt" is vital in the event the adoption is ever legally questioned

- Read the client's acknowledgement out loud to the petitioner, and have the client affirm the petition in front of a notary. Maintain a strong working relationship with your local adoption case workers and civil department.

- Have an attorney represent the birth mother in cases of adoption. Ensure that the attorney meets with the mother and reviews her rights. Also, have that attorney sign documentation showing that advice was given and the right to revoke was explained.

Brian W. King is the senior partner and managing attorney of King Law Offices, PLLC. He has been practicing law for more than a decade, and is a lifelong resident of Rutherford County, North Carolina. Mr. King is a member of the North and South Carolina bars, and maintains active cases and appeals in both states. He is a graduate of Campbell Law School and completed his undergraduate degree at University of North Carolina at Charlotte. In 2009, Mr. King became a North Carolina Certified Family Law Specialist.

In addition to maintaining a busy private practice, Mr. King has served as a contracted attorney for the Departments of Social Service. He has also served as a member of the North Carolina Child Support Council and has presented numerous continued legal education classes, including case reviews classes on new and developing law. Mr. King has been elected as president of the Judicial District Bar, and has served in various legal leadership positions.

Acknowledgment: *I would like to thank Joshua Mooring at Appalachian School of Law, Kassia Walker and Jade Davis of Charlotte School of Law for their aid in this chapter. They have provided an excellent research background for this chapter, along with the personal touch of working with cases in our firm. A special thank you goes out to my law firm staff, each person providing the nuts and bolts of every adoption that goes through our office.*

Third Party Assisted Reproduction: Assisting Couples Amidst the Changing Legal Landscape

Tim Schlesinger

Shareholder

Paule Camazine & Blumenthal PC

ASPATORE

Third Party Assisted Reproduction: Assisting Couples Amidst the Changing Legal Landscape

Tim Schlesinger

Shareholder

Paule Camazine & Blumenthal PC

ASPATORE

Introduction

I am a partner at a twenty-eight-lawyer firm with a large family law practice in St. Louis, Missouri. We have twelve full-time family law attorneys in this firm. My family law practice evolved as a traditional family law practice, revolving mostly around complex divorce and family law litigation, but about ten years ago I began to get involved in third party assisted reproduction practice. This includes surrogacy, egg donations, embryo donations, sperm donations, and parties wishing to reproduce using in vitro fertilization (IVF) or other technological means—basically any situation involving anyone needing the assistance of third parties who are not going to be the parent of the child.

While working in this field is challenging, it is truly rewarding to help clients build their families instead of dealing with the breakup of families. It is a very narrow field—there are only a handful of lawyers in the St. Louis area who consistently deal with third party assisted reproduction. The initial challenge was just trying to learn about it and finding the work. This process took several years.

Technological, Sociological Impacts on Third Party Assisted Reproduction

The technology involved in third party assisted reproduction (although commonly referred to as Assisted Reproductive Technology (ART), I prefer not to use it as it is a completely baffling acronym to those not familiar with it) has taken a big leap in the last few years. The process of freezing eggs and embryos keeps improving, along with increased success rates for live births as a result of third party assisted reproduction. In vitro fertilization (IVF) technology is only thirty-six years old—it has improved greatly since then, and it will only continue to do so. This is resulting in more prospective parents seeking these types of fertility treatments, and bringing me a much larger workload. Staying up to date with the technology is very important—I have to continue to educate myself through attending conferences, exchanging information with attorneys in the same field, and streamlining my practice to be able to focus on assisted reproduction so I can enable myself to give the best advice to my surrogacy and other assisted reproduction clients as possible.

The evolution of our societal norms in the last several years has also increased public knowledge and use of third party assisted reproduction. First, people are having children later in life, which impacts their ability to have a natural pregnancy and birth. There are more health risks in childbirth, for women, as they age. In addition, women's ability to produce viable eggs (statistically) drops significantly after age thirty-five. As a result, it is often more viable to use ART for those seeking to have children later in life. Second, there is a greater acceptance of non-traditional families and non-traditional ways of having birth amongst the younger generations coming up today. It was far less common for same-sex couples to raise children twenty years ago than it is today. The increasing acceptance by society at large of same-sex marriage and same-sex couples raising children has dramatically increased the need for third party assisted reproduction in the same-sex community. These societal shifts, in hand with the vastly improved technology, have made ART far more viable in this age.

Surrogacy Cases Involving Same-Sex Parents

There are inherent special considerations involved in surrogacy cases with same-sex parents. First, one of the parents will not be genetically related to the child and, depending on what state you live in, this can impact the legal proceedings necessary to become a legal parent. I practice primarily in Missouri and Illinois, and the procedures are completely different in each of these states. The Illinois Gestation Surrogacy Act is, in my opinion, the most surrogacy-friendly statute in the country.[1] It allows people who comply with the requirements of the statute to enter into a surrogacy arrangement, for compensation or not, as long as the surrogate and the intended parents comply with the requirements of the statute. When the child is born, the birth certificate is issued with the names of the intended parents as long as the appropriate affidavits are filed with the Illinois Department of Health. In my view, there is nothing in the act that prohibits same-sex couples from using the Act and reaping its benefits.

In Missouri, there is no codified law regarding surrogacy. There are no statutes and no case law. As a result, practitioners in this field must use existing parentage and adoption laws to accomplish the goal of any

---

[1] 750 ILCS 47/1 et seq.

surrogacy arrangement—exclusive legal and physical parentage for the intended parents. For example, suppose a gay male couple has a child through a surrogate using the sperm of one of the men. The other is not biologically related to the child, so when the child is born only the genetically related father will be on the birth certificate—the other will have to adopt the child under Missouri law. This is not an automatic process—you must be aware of where you are. There may be certain jurisdictions in the state in which the judges will not necessarily be amenable to such an arrangement. As a practitioner, you have to have or acquire that knowledge, so that you can give intelligent advice to the client. It is important to discuss these issues with the client at the beginning of the process to ensure that it will go smoothly. In some jurisdictions, these types of adoptions are handled the same way that stepparent adoptions are, and it is fairly routine. The birth mother is still the presumed birth mother under Missouri law, and under the law of every state, so her parental rights must be terminated. This must be done by consent and must be very specifically and unambiguously set forth in a surrogacy agreement drafted on behalf of the parties.

The surrogacy agreement must be written and executed before the child is conceived. If the child is born and there is no agreement in place, you leave yourself and your clients open to all manner of mischief and potentially devastating results. In Illinois, the surrogacy agreement must be completed and executed before medical procedures begin, in order to comply with the statute. The gestational carrier cannot be genetically related to the child and one of the two intended parents has to provide a gamete. The actual surrogacy agreement has to have certain specific things in it. If those requirements are met, affidavits are filed when the child is born, the birth certificate is issued, and no further legal action needs to be taken to create legal parentage. If the statute is not complied with, the practitioner is left using the same mechanisms of parentage and adoption as are used in Missouri.

Working with Surrogacy Clients

More often than not, people already have a surrogate when they come to me, but people do frequently seek my counsel at the beginning of the surrogacy process, before they have found or even begun looking for a surrogate. My involvement becomes more critical after a surrogate has been chosen. I do need to know their relationship with the surrogate. I also want to know about the intended parents' relationship, and whether it is stable. On the one hand it is not my business—these people are adults making their own decisions—but I do not want people, for example, that have been dating each other for nine months to come to me and say they want to have a child through a surrogate. That is the kind of thing I would probably counsel against. I also need to know what they contemplate in terms of genetic relationship between the child and the surrogate.

Traditional Surrogacy

Every once in a while I have someone come to me intending to have a traditional surrogacy. This occurs when the surrogate is artificially inseminated with the sperm of one of the intended parents, and as a result, the surrogate is both the birth mother and the genetic mother of the child. I do not generally support this strategy. I am reasonably certain that states with gestational surrogacy statutes do not cover traditional surrogacy. The problem with using a traditional surrogate in any state that does not have an unambiguous statute that includes traditional surrogacy is that the surrogate has a far superior right to the child that is born than the intended parent who is not genetically related to the child.

The infamous *Baby M* case illustrates this well: The Sterns, a married couple, contracted with Mary Beth Whitehead to have a traditional surrogacy, and it was very clear from the agreement that she was supposed to give up this child and the Sterns were supposed to raise it.[2] Whitehead was inseminated with sperm from Mr. Stern, became pregnant, and was paid for carrying the child. When the baby was born, Mary Beth Whitehead became depressed and begged the Sterns to let her have the child for a week before giving it up. She then took the child and fled to Florida. The sheriffs tracked her down, where they caught her climbing out of a window with the baby. Three years of litigation over the custody of the child resulted from this unfortunate scenario. Ultimately, Mr. Stern was awarded custody of the child, but Mrs. Stern had no theoretical custody rights at all. If Mary Beth Whitehead had been a more stable person, she would have had a pretty

---

[2] *Matter of Baby M,* 109 N.J. 396, 537 A.2d 1227 (1988).

good chance of getting custody of the child as the genetic parent. I always tell my potential clients that traditional surrogacy is a terrible idea. I have never actually handled a traditional surrogacy case, and I would only do it under extreme circumstances—the legal risks to the intended parents are just far too great.

Things to Consider Before Deciding on a Surrogacy Plan

When I counsel clients on pursuing a surrogacy plan, I make sure that they consider several issues that they may need to address down the road. They must consider how they know the surrogate, their relationship with her, how they found her, and the level of trust they have for her. They must consider where this child is going to be born—due to the importance of the laws surrounding their particular circumstances and the jurisdiction that will be administering the law. If I am counseling people who live in or even near Illinois, I tell them to try to have the child born in Illinois so they can take advantage of the Illinois Gestational Surrogacy Act.[3] I also tell them to try to find a surrogate who actually lives in Illinois, as this will simplify the process even more so.

Selecting a surrogate is a crucial piece of the puzzle as well. You usually want to have a surrogate who has already had a child—if they have not had a child, there is a greater chance they will become too attached during the pregnancy and cause problems down the road. Additionally, I think it is almost exploitative to have a gestational carrier who has never had a child—it is a requirement of the Illinois Gestational Surrogacy Act for the surrogate to already have had a child.

There are agencies that provide couples looking for a surrogate with people who are willing to do so. Many people have sisters or other friends or relatives that act as their surrogates. Using a relative has positive and negative aspects; on one hand, it is very helpful for intended parents to have a surrogate they already know and trust. That makes the surrogacy process much less nerve-wracking for the intended parents. On the other hand, if the surrogate is a family member or close friend, then everyone must deal with the complication of what you tell a child, when you tell

---

[3] 750 ILCS 47/1 *et seq.*

them, and how that affects them when they know the person who carried them was not the person they consider their mother. They must also deal with feelings of attachment the surrogate may have for a child they carried.

I do not take part in connecting people with surrogates—that is not the job of the lawyer, nor should it be. I give people suggestions and contact information for agencies. There are plenty of programs that connect intended parents with surrogates, and my job is to facilitate the agreement between the parties once they are before me.

Preparing and Processing the Surrogacy Agreement

The most important provisions in the agreements and documentation that I provide for the parties are also the most simple and straightforward. They must state unequivocally and unambiguously without a doubt that the child belongs to the intended parents and that the gestational carrier or surrogate has no rights and no obligations with regard to any child that is born. The surrogate has no input, no say, no choice, no connection with the raising of the child—period. The intended parents have the only rights and the only obligations, regarding any child that is born. That is what I tell people when they are sitting down with me and ask what needs to be in the agreement. I tell them that this language is there to achieve what they are trying to accomplish and it is the most important thing in the agreement. I repeat this language over and over again—its needs to be undeniably clear.

Achieving Legal Parentage

There are two primary methods in which courts process a surrogacy agreement to achieve the result that the intended parents are the sole legal parents of the child. The first is what is generally called a second parent adoption. This usually involves a same-sex couple, one of which is a genetic parent, and an outside genetic parent who is not going to be involved in raising the child. The Missouri adoption statute and the adoption statutes of many other states essentially say that the parental rights of the genetic parents have to be terminated normally for the child to be adopted. However, when one of the genetic parents is also one of the intended parents, you obviously do not want to terminate the parental rights of both genetic parents. We call this situation of a second intended parent adopting in addition to the existing intended genetic parent, a second parent adoption. The one exception to this rule that exists in the adoption statute is for stepparent adoption. (If gay marriage were legal in Missouri, second parent adoptions would simply be stepparent adoptions in cases where the same-sex couples were married.) Under current law, practitioners have to find jurisdictions that will not object to same-sex couples adopting children. In these jurisdictions, we simply treat the adopting partner procedurally as if he or she were a stepparent. Beginning in June, gay marriage will be legal in Illinois, so this type of adoption will not be difficult to process there once the statute is effective—this is another example of the importance of knowing the different laws in different jurisdictions in these cases.

Legal issues that may seem novel to the courts arise in surrogacy cases involving heterosexual couples as well. For example, a married heterosexual couple had twins through a surrogate. They were both the genetic parents, they used their own gametes, created embryos, and the embryos were implanted in the surrogate. The surrogate had the babies in a rural county in Missouri, where the intended mother was a lawyer. In this situation, I represented the surrogate so the genetic mother could represent herself when it came time to file the actions she needed to be declared the legal parents of the children. They filed an action under the Uniform Parentage Act (UPA) to have themselves declared legal and genetic parents. She went to court and did all the things I told her to do, presented the necessary affidavits from the doctors explaining how the children were born, and so on. The judge did not understand how the UPA applied, and originally insisted that the genetic mother should have access to the twins, even though she was the genetic mother. As the attorney for the surrogate, I was able to travel to the jurisdiction and explain to the judge that the UPA allowed him to enter a judgment declaring the intended mother, who was also the genetic mother, to be the legal mother. This is an example of how each set of facts is different, and this was the easiest way to resolve the problem in this circumstance.

Because traditional surrogacy is so rare and gestational carriers are the norm in surrogacy cases, it is very rare for the carrier to try to retain their rights to the child and keep it away from the intended parents. I will only deal with a gestational carrier who is not the genetic mother and who also already has at least one child to avoid these situations. Although it is possible for a gestational carrier to try to assert custody or parentage rights, and I do tell my clients this (especially in a state like Missouri where there is no statute or case law), it is very unlikely because the gestational carriers in these cases do not want to raise children—that is not why they are doing this.

The Surrogate's Motivation

It is very common that these surrogates get something emotionally out of helping someone else build their family. I know we live in a very cynical world, and the surrogates are often compensated handsomely, but I really do not think the motivation is primarily monetary. Pregnancy is a lot to go through for money—the national average costs of paying a surrogate are between twenty and thirty thousand dollars; there are other ways to make that kind of money.

In some states, such as Arizona, Michigan, New York, Indiana, North Dakota, and Washington, DC, compensating a surrogate is illegal. In Michigan, for example, it is a felony to participate in a compensated surrogacy arrangement. You have to be very careful and counsel your clients about insulating themselves from potential liability if they have connections to or reside in states in which surrogacy is illegal.

Conclusion

The evolution of assisted reproductive technology and its relationship to the evolution of our societal norms in the last two decades, in particular, has increased the knowledge about and use of third party assisted reproduction. Surrogacies become more common, as the technology for creating and freezing embryos improves, and as the need for surrogacy increases as a tool to solve fertility problems, for single parents, heterosexual couples, and same-sex couples. Surrogacy as a legal field is a fluid and dynamic area in which the playing field is constantly changing and the stakes are enormously high for the clients.

If you are a family law attorney aspiring to work in the surrogacy fields, I think the most important thing you can do is educate yourself. Go to conferences; get involved in the organizations, such as the American Bar Association, Family Law Section Assisted Reproduction Committee, just to name one.

Take the time to educate yourself before you start representing people because there are a lot of pitfalls. You need to understand more than just the custody and parentage issues. The potential legal and financial consequences, as well as the insurance issues, are critical to giving your clients intelligent, comprehensive legal advice in this area. Most of all, you need to care about your clients. To be successful in this fluid and dynamic field, you need to be open minded, willing to learn, and willing to spend the time to continue learning.

The role of *counselor* is crucial here; people who come to seek guidance from you do so in an extremely vulnerable emotional state. They are coming to you in hopes of creating a family due to fertility issues. Or perhaps they are a same-sex couple trying to navigate the minefield of creating a legal family in a society that does not make it easy to do so. You need to understand the circumstances of your clients' particular situation and what your clients are attempting to achieve, and care about the results.

Key Takeaways

- Third party assisted reproduction has become significantly more common in recent years due primarily to three factors: the improved technology making it possible, the increased age of individuals interested in parenthood that are not physically able to carry out pregnancy, and the rising number of same-sex couples looking to start families.

- Traditional surrogacy is a very risky strategy for the intended parents—the surrogate mother will often become more attached to the baby because it is actually their own, and the surrogate mother may have a very strong legal argument for custody if they change their mind and decide they want custody. For these reasons, I strongly advise against any intended parents using the traditional surrogacy method.

- The most important provisions in the agreements and documentation that I provide for the parties are also the most simple and straightforward. They must state unequivocally and unambiguously that the child belongs to the intended parents and that the gestational carrier or surrogate has no rights and no obligations with regard to any child born as the result of the surrogacy.

- Second parent adoptions are a legal grey area these days when it comes to same-sex couples. As more and more states legalize same-sex marriage and allow for same-sex couples to adopt as stepparents, this legal grey area will gradually diminish.

Tim Schlesinger is a shareholder in the firm of Paule Camazine & Blumenthal PC. He received his undergraduate degree in journalism from University of Missouri-Columbia in 1979, and his JD from University of Missouri-Columbia in 1983. Since 1993, Mr. Schlesinger has practiced almost exclusively in family law, including the representation of people in third party assisted reproduction. He is licensed to practice in Missouri and Illinois, is a member of the Assisted Reproduction Committee of the Family Law Section of the American Bar Association, and is a member of the American Society for Reproductive Medicine–Legal Professionals Division. Mr. Schlesinger is the author of Chapter 30, Family Law Deskbook, Alternative Means of Reproduction, The Missouri Bar (7th Ed. 2012); Assisted Human Reproduction: Unsolved Issues in Parentage, Child Custody and Support, 61 J.Mo.Bar 22 (2005); and Surrogacy and Egg Donation Agreements - The Search for Certainty in an Uncertain Field, 59 St. Louis Bar J.28 (2013).

APPENDICES

APPENDIX A

THE HAGUE CONVENTION

33. CONVENTION ON PROTECTION OF CHILDREN AND CO-OPERATION IN RESPECT OF INTERCOUNTRY ADOPTION[1]

(Concluded 29 May 1993)

The States signatory to the present Convention,

Recognising that the child, for the full and harmonious development of his or her personality, should grow up in a family environment, in an atmosphere of happiness, love and understanding,

Recalling that each State should take, as a matter of priority, appropriate measures to enable the child to remain in the care of his or her family of origin,

Recognising that intercountry adoption may offer the advantage of a permanent family to a child for whom a suitable family cannot be found in his or her State of origin,

Convinced of the necessity to take measures to ensure that intercountry adoptions are made in the best interests of the child and with respect for his or her fundamental rights, and to prevent the abduction, the sale of, or traffic in children,

Desiring to establish common provisions to this effect, taking into account the principles set forth in international instruments, in particular the *United Nations Convention on the Rights of the Child*, of 20 November 1989, and the United Nations Declaration on Social and Legal Principles relating to the Protection and Welfare of Children, with Special Reference to Foster Placement and Adoption Nationally and Internationally (General Assembly Resolution 41/85, of 3 December 1986),

Have agreed upon the following provisions –

CHAPTER I – SCOPE OF THE CONVENTION

Article 1

The objects of the present Convention are –

a)   to establish safeguards to ensure that intercountry adoptions take place in the best interests of the child and with respect for his or her fundamental rights as recognised in international law;

b)   to establish a system of co-operation amongst Contracting States to ensure that those safeguards are respected and thereby prevent the abduction, the sale of, or traffic in children;

c)   to secure the recognition in Contracting States of adoptions made in accordance with the Convention.

Article 2

(1)   The Convention shall apply where a child habitually resident in one Contracting State ("the State of origin") has been, is being, or is to be moved to another Contracting State ("the receiving State") either after his or her adoption in the State of origin by spouses or a person habitually resident in the receiving State, or for the purposes of such an adoption in the receiving State or in the State of origin.

(2)   The Convention covers only adoptions which create a permanent parent-child relationship.

---

[1] This Convention, including related materials, is accessible on the website of the Hague Conference on Private International Law (www.hcch.net), under "Conventions" or under the "Intercountry Adoption Section". For the full history of the Convention, see Hague Conference on Private International Law, *Proceedings of the Seventeenth Session (1993)*, Tome II, *Adoption – co-operation* (ISBN 90 399 0782 X, 659 pp.).

Article 4

An adoption within the scope of the Convention shall take place only if the competent authorities of the State of origin –

a)   have established that the child is adoptable;

b)   have determined, after possibilities for placement of the child within the State of origin have been given due consideration, that an intercountry adoption is in the child's best interests;

c)   have ensured that

    (1)   the persons, institutions and authorities whose consent is necessary for adoption, have been counselled as may be necessary and duly informed of the effects of their consent, in particular whether or not an adoption will result in the termination of the legal relationship between the child and his or her family of origin,

    (2)   such persons, institutions and authorities have given their consent freely, in the required legal form, and expressed or evidenced in writing,

    (3)   the consents have not been induced by payment or compensation of any kind and have not been withdrawn, and

    (4)   the consent of the mother, where required, has been given only after the birth of the child; and

d)   have ensured, having regard to the age and degree of maturity of the child, that

    (1)   he or she has been counselled and duly informed of the effects of the adoption and of his or her consent to the adoption, where such consent is required,

    (2)   consideration has been given to the child's wishes and opinions,

    (3)   the child's consent to the adoption, where such consent is required, has been given freely, in the required legal form, and expressed or evidenced in writing, and

    (4)   such consent has not been induced by payment or compensation of any kind.

Article 5

An adoption within the scope of the Convention shall take place only if the competent authorities of the receiving State –

a)   have determined that the prospective adoptive parents are eligible and suited to adopt;

b)   have ensured that the prospective adoptive parents have been counselled as may be necessary; and

c)   have determined that the child is or will be authorised to enter and reside permanently in that State.

CHAPTER III – CENTRAL AUTHORITIES AND ACCREDITED BODIES

Article 6

(1)   A Contracting State shall designate a Central Authority to discharge the duties which are imposed by the Convention upon such authorities.

(2)   Federal States, States with more than one system of law or States having autonomous territorial units shall be free to appoint more than one Central Authority and to specify the territorial or personal extent of their functions. Where a State has appointed more than one Central Authority, it shall designate the Central Authority to which any communication may be addressed for transmission to the appropriate Central Authority within that State.

Article 7

(1)   Central Authorities shall co-operate with each other and promote co-operation amongst the competent authorities in their States to protect children and to achieve the other objects of the Convention.

(2)   They shall take directly all appropriate measures to –
        a)   provide information as to the laws of their States concerning adoption and other general information, such as statistics and standard forms;
        b)   keep one another informed about the operation of the Convention and, as far as possible, eliminate any obstacles to its application.

Article 8

Central Authorities shall take, directly or through public authorities, all appropriate measures to prevent improper financial or other gain in connection with an adoption and to deter all practices contrary to the objects of the Convention.

Article 9

Central Authorities shall take, directly or through public authorities or other bodies duly accredited in their State, all appropriate measures, in particular to –
a)   collect, preserve and exchange information about the situation of the child and the prospective adoptive parents, so far as is necessary to complete the adoption;
b)   facilitate, follow and expedite proceedings with a view to obtaining the adoption;
c)   promote the development of adoption counselling and post-adoption services in their States;
d)   provide each other with general evaluation reports about experience with intercountry adoption;
e)   reply, in so far as is permitted by the law of their State, to justified requests from other Central Authorities or public authorities for information about a particular adoption situation.

Article 10

Accreditation shall only be granted to and maintained by bodies demonstrating their competence to carry out properly the tasks with which they may be entrusted.

Article 11

An accredited body shall –
a)   pursue only non-profit objectives according to such conditions and within such limits as may be established by the competent authorities of the State of accreditation;
b)   be directed and staffed by persons qualified by their ethical standards and by training or experience to work in the field of intercountry adoption; and
c)   be subject to supervision by competent authorities of that State as to its composition, operation and financial situation.

Article 12

A body accredited in one Contracting State may act in another Contracting State only if the competent authorities of both States have authorised it to do so.

Article 13

The designation of the Central Authorities and, where appropriate, the extent of their functions, as well as the names and addresses of the accredited bodies shall be communicated by each Contracting State to the Permanent Bureau of the Hague Conference on Private International Law.

CHAPTER IV – PROCEDURAL REQUIREMENTS IN INTERCOUNTRY ADOPTION

Article 14

Persons habitually resident in a Contracting State, who wish to adopt a child habitually resident in another Contracting State, shall apply to the Central Authority in the State of their habitual residence.

Article 15

(1)   If the Central Authority of the receiving State is satisfied that the applicants are eligible and suited to adopt, it shall prepare a report including information about their identity, eligibility and suitability to adopt, background, family and medical history, social environment, reasons for adoption, ability to undertake an intercountry adoption, as well as the characteristics of the children for whom they would be qualified to care.

(2)   It shall transmit the report to the Central Authority of the State of origin.

Article 16

(1)   If the Central Authority of the State of origin is satisfied that the child is adoptable, it shall –
   a)   prepare a report including information about his or her identity, adoptability, background, social environment, family history, medical history including that of the child's family, and any special needs of the child;
   b)   give due consideration to the child's upbringing and to his or her ethnic, religious and cultural background;
   c)   ensure that consents have been obtained in accordance with Article 4; and
   d)   determine, on the basis in particular of the reports relating to the child and the prospective adoptive parents, whether the envisaged placement is in the best interests of the child.

(2)   It shall transmit to the Central Authority of the receiving State its report on the child, proof that the necessary consents have been obtained and the reasons for its determination on the placement, taking care not to reveal the identity of the mother and the father if, in the State of origin, these identities may not be disclosed.

Article 17

Any decision in the State of origin that a child should be entrusted to prospective adoptive parents may only be made if –
   a)   the Central Authority of that State has ensured that the prospective adoptive parents agree;
   b)   the Central Authority of the receiving State has approved such decision, where such approval is required by the law of that State or by the Central Authority of the State of origin;
   c)   the Central Authorities of both States have agreed that the adoption may proceed; and
   d)   it has been determined, in accordance with Article 5, that the prospective adoptive parents are eligible and suited to adopt and that the child is or will be authorised to enter and reside permanently in the receiving State.

Article 18

The Central Authorities of both States shall take all necessary steps to obtain permission for the child to leave the State of origin and to enter and reside permanently in the receiving State.

Article 19

(1)   The transfer of the child to the receiving State may only be carried out if the requirements of Article 17 have been satisfied.

(2)   The Central Authorities of both States shall ensure that this transfer takes place in secure and appropriate circumstances and, if possible, in the company of the adoptive or prospective adoptive parents.

(3)   If the transfer of the child does not take place, the reports referred to in Articles 15 and 16 are to be sent back to the authorities who forwarded them.

Article 20

The Central Authorities shall keep each other informed about the adoption process and the measures taken to complete it, as well as about the progress of the placement if a probationary period is required.

Article 21

(1)   Where the adoption is to take place after the transfer of the child to the receiving State and it appears to the Central Authority of that State that the continued placement of the child with the prospective adoptive parents is not in the child's best interests, such Central Authority shall take the measures necessary to protect the child, in particular –
    a)   to cause the child to be withdrawn from the prospective adoptive parents and to arrange temporary care;
    b)   in consultation with the Central Authority of the State of origin, to arrange without delay a new placement of the child with a view to adoption or, if this is not appropriate, to arrange alternative long-term care; an adoption shall not take place until the Central Authority of the State of origin has been duly informed concerning the new prospective adoptive parents;
    c)   as a last resort, to arrange the return of the child, if his or her interests so require.
(2)   Having regard in particular to the age and degree of maturity of the child, he or she shall be consulted and, where appropriate, his or her consent obtained in relation to measures to be taken under this Article.

Article 22

(1)   The functions of a Central Authority under this Chapter may be performed by public authorities or by bodies accredited under Chapter III, to the extent permitted by the law of its State.
(2)   Any Contracting State may declare to the depositary of the Convention that the functions of the Central Authority under Articles 15 to 21 may be performed in that State, to the extent permitted by the law and subject to the supervision of the competent authorities of that State, also by bodies or persons who –
    a)   meet the requirements of integrity, professional competence, experience and accountability of that State; and
    b)   are qualified by their ethical standards and by training or experience to work in the field of intercountry adoption.
(3)   A Contracting State which makes the declaration provided for in paragraph 2 shall keep the Permanent Bureau of the Hague Conference on Private International Law informed of the names and addresses of these bodies and persons.
(4)   Any Contracting State may declare to the depositary of the Convention that adoptions of children habitually resident in its territory may only take place if the functions of the Central Authorities are performed in accordance with paragraph 1.
(5)   Notwithstanding any declaration made under paragraph 2, the reports provided for in Articles 15 and 16 shall, in every case, be prepared under the responsibility of the Central Authority or other authorities or bodies in accordance with paragraph 1.

CHAPTER V – RECOGNITION AND EFFECTS OF THE ADOPTION

Article 23

(1)   An adoption certified by the competent authority of the State of the adoption as having been made in accordance with the Convention shall be recognised by operation of law in the other Contracting States. The certificate shall specify when and by whom the agreements under Article 17, sub-paragraph c), were given.

(2)   Each Contracting State shall, at the time of signature, ratification, acceptance, approval or accession, notify the depositary of the Convention of the identity and the functions of the authority or the authorities which, in that State, are competent to make the certification. It shall also notify the depositary of any modification in the designation of these authorities.

Article 24

The recognition of an adoption may be refused in a Contracting State only if the adoption is manifestly contrary to its public policy, taking into account the best interests of the child.

Article 25

Any Contracting State may declare to the depositary of the Convention that it will not be bound under this Convention to recognise adoptions made in accordance with an agreement concluded by application of Article 39, paragraph 2.

Article 26

(1)   The recognition of an adoption includes recognition of
   a)   the legal parent-child relationship between the child and his or her adoptive parents;
   b)   parental responsibility of the adoptive parents for the child;
   c)   the termination of a pre-existing legal relationship between the child and his or her mother and father, if the adoption has this effect in the Contracting State where it was made.
(2)   In the case of an adoption having the effect of terminating a pre-existing legal parent-child relationship, the child shall enjoy in the receiving State, and in any other Contracting State where the adoption is recognised, rights equivalent to those resulting from adoptions having this effect in each such State.
(3)   The preceding paragraphs shall not prejudice the application of any provision more favourable for the child, in force in the Contracting State which recognises the adoption.

Article 27

(1)   Where an adoption granted in the State of origin does not have the effect of terminating a pre-existing legal parent-child relationship, it may, in the receiving State which recognises the adoption under the Convention, be converted into an adoption having such an effect –
   a)   if the law of the receiving State so permits; and
   b)   if the consents referred to in Article 4, sub-paragraphs c and d, have been or are given for the purpose of such an adoption.
(2)   Article 23 applies to the decision converting the adoption.

CHAPTER VI – GENERAL PROVISIONS

Article 28

The Convention does not affect any law of a State of origin which requires that the adoption of a child habitually resident within that State take place in that State or which prohibits the child's placement in, or transfer to, the receiving State prior to adoption.

Article 29

There shall be no contact between the prospective adoptive parents and the child's parents or any other person who has care of the child until the requirements of Article 4, sub-paragraphs a) to c), and Article 5, sub-paragraph a), have been met, unless the adoption takes place within a family or unless the contact is in compliance with the conditions established by the competent authority of the State of origin.

Article 30

(1) The competent authorities of a Contracting State shall ensure that information held by them concerning the child's origin, in particular information concerning the identity of his or her parents, as well as the medical history, is preserved.
(2) They shall ensure that the child or his or her representative has access to such information, under appropriate guidance, in so far as is permitted by the law of that State.

Article 31

Without prejudice to Article 30, personal data gathered or transmitted under the Convention, especially data referred to in Articles 15 and 16, shall be used only for the purposes for which they were gathered or transmitted.

Article 32

(1) No one shall derive improper financial or other gain from an activity related to an intercountry adoption.
(2) Only costs and expenses, including reasonable professional fees of persons involved in the adoption, may be charged or paid.
(3) The directors, administrators and employees of bodies involved in an adoption shall not receive remuneration which is unreasonably high in relation to services rendered.

Article 33

A competent authority which finds that any provision of the Convention has not been respected or that there is a serious risk that it may not be respected, shall immediately inform the Central Authority of its State. This Central Authority shall be responsible for ensuring that appropriate measures are taken.

Article 34

If the competent authority of the State of destination of a document so requests, a translation certified as being in conformity with the original must be furnished. Unless otherwise provided, the costs of such translation are to be borne by the prospective adoptive parents.

Article 35

The competent authorities of the Contracting States shall act expeditiously in the process of adoption.

Article 36

In relation to a State which has two or more systems of law with regard to adoption applicable in different territorial units –
a) any reference to habitual residence in that State shall be construed as referring to habitual residence in a territorial unit of that State;
b) any reference to the law of that State shall be construed as referring to the law in force in the relevant territorial unit;
c) any reference to the competent authorities or to the public authorities of that State shall be construed as referring to those authorised to act in the relevant territorial unit;
d) any reference to the accredited bodies of that State shall be construed as referring to bodies accredited in the relevant territorial unit.

Article 37

In relation to a State which with regard to adoption has two or more systems of law applicable to different categories of persons, any reference to the law of that State shall be construed as referring to the legal system specified by the law of that State.

Article 38

A State within which different territorial units have their own rules of law in respect of adoption shall not be bound to apply the Convention where a State with a unified system of law would not be bound to do so.

Article 39

(1)   The Convention does not affect any international instrument to which Contracting States are Parties and which contains provisions on matters governed by the Convention, unless a contrary declaration is made by the States Parties to such instrument.

(2)   Any Contracting State may enter into agreements with one or more other Contracting States, with a view to improving the application of the Convention in their mutual relations. These agreements may derogate only from the provisions of Articles 14 to 16 and 18 to 21. The States which have concluded such an agreement shall transmit a copy to the depositary of the Convention.

Article 40

No reservation to the Convention shall be permitted.

Article 41

The Convention shall apply in every case where an application pursuant to Article 14 has been received after the Convention has entered into force in the receiving State and the State of origin.

Article 42

The Secretary General of the Hague Conference on Private International Law shall at regular intervals convene a Special Commission in order to review the practical operation of the Convention.

CHAPTER VII – FINAL CLAUSES

Article 43

(1)   The Convention shall be open for signature by the States which were Members of the Hague Conference on Private International Law at the time of its Seventeenth Session and by the other States which participated in that Session.

(2)   It shall be ratified, accepted or approved and the instruments of ratification, acceptance or approval shall be deposited with the Ministry of Foreign Affairs of the Kingdom of the Netherlands, depositary of the Convention.

Article 44

(1)   Any other State may accede to the Convention after it has entered into force in accordance with Article 46, paragraph 1.

(2)   The instrument of accession shall be deposited with the depositary.

(3)   Such accession shall have effect only as regards the relations between the acceding State and those Contracting States which have not raised an objection to its accession in the six months

after the receipt of the notification referred to in sub-paragraph *b)* of Article 48. Such an objection may also be raised by States at the time when they ratify, accept or approve the Convention after an accession. Any such objection shall be notified to the depositary.

Article 45

(1) If a State has two or more territorial units in which different systems of law are applicable in relation to matters dealt with in the Convention, it may at the time of signature, ratification, acceptance, approval or accession declare that this Convention shall extend to all its territorial units or only to one or more of them and may modify this declaration by submitting another declaration at any time.
(2) Any such declaration shall be notified to the depositary and shall state expressly the territorial units to which the Convention applies.
(3) If a State makes no declaration under this Article, the Convention is to extend to all territorial units of that State.

Article 46

(1) The Convention shall enter into force on the first day of the month following the expiration of three months after the deposit of the third instrument of ratification, acceptance or approval referred to in Article 43.
(2) Thereafter the Convention shall enter into force –
    a)   for each State ratifying, accepting or approving it subsequently, or acceding to it, on the first day of the month following the expiration of three months after the deposit of its instrument of ratification, acceptance, approval or accession;
    b)   for a territorial unit to which the Convention has been extended in conformity with Article 45, on the first day of the month following the expiration of three months after the notification referred to in that Article.

Article 47

(1) A State Party to the Convention may denounce it by a notification in writing addressed to the depositary.
(2) The denunciation takes effect on the first day of the month following the expiration of twelve months after the notification is received by the depositary. Where a longer period for the denunciation to take effect is specified in the notification, the denunciation takes effect upon the expiration of such longer period after the notification is received by the depositary.

Article 48

The depositary shall notify the States Members of the Hague Conference on Private International Law, the other States which participated in the Seventeenth Session and the States which have acceded in accordance with Article 44, of the following –
a) the signatures, ratifications, acceptances and approvals referred to in Article 43;
b) the accessions and objections raised to accessions referred to in Article 44;
c) the date on which the Convention enters into force in accordance with Article 46;
d) the declarations and designations referred to in Articles 22, 23, 25 and 45;
e) the agreements referred to in Article 39;
f) the denunciations referred to in Article 47.

In witness whereof the undersigned, being duly authorised thereto, have signed this Convention.

Done at The Hague, on the 29th day of May 1993, in the English and French languages, both texts being equally authentic, in a single copy which shall be deposited in the archives of the Government of the Kingdom of the Netherlands, and of which a certified copy shall be sent, through diplomatic channels, to each of the States Members of the Hague Conference on Private International Law at the date of its Seventeenth Session and to each of the other States which participated in that Session.

Courtesy of Karen K. Greenberg, Konowitz & Greenberg

APPENDIX B

LIST OF RESEARCH SOURCES

Relevant Websites

- https://www.childwelfare.gov/pubs/f_start.cfm#understand
- http://www.nolo.com/legal-encyclopedia/adoption-procedures-30201.html
- http://www.adoptionchildwelfarelaw.org/document_detail.php?id=2138
- http://www.adoptionchildwelfarelaw.org/document_detail.php?id=961
- Adoption & Child Welfare LawSite—North Carolina Case Summary/Adoption, http://www.adoptionchildwelfarelaw.org/document_detail.php?id=961 (last visited March 11, 2014).
- Interstate Compact on the Placement of Children (ICPC) http://www.aphsa.org/content/AAICPC/en/home.html

Relevant Statutory References

- N.C. Gen. Stat. Ann. § 49A-1
- N.C. Gen. Stat. Ann. § 49A-1.
- N.C. Gen. Stat. Ann. §48-10-103
- N.C. Gen. Stat. Ann. § 48-10-103.
- N.C. Gen. Stat. Ann..§48-3-601
- N.C. Gen. Stat. Ann..§48-3-608
- N.C. Gen. Stat. Ann. § 48-3-608

Relevant Caselaw

- *Petersen v. Rogers*, 111 N.C. App. 712, 713, 433 S.E.2d 770 , 772 (1993)
- *Price v. Howard*, 346 N.C. 68, 484 S.E.2d 528 (1997)

Relevant Analytical Research Sources

- Lee's North Carolina Family Law
- <u>Child Welfare Information Gateway</u>. (2011). *Postadoption contract agreements between birth and adoptive families.* Washington, DC: U.S. Department of Health and Human Services, Children's Bureau.

Courtesy of Brian W. King, King Crotts Duncan & Jaynes

APPENDIX C

US SURROGACY LAW—JURISDICTION BY JURISDICTION

ALABAMA
There is no law (case law or statutory) specifically allowing or prohibiting surrogacy agreements.

ALASKA
There is no law (case law or statutory) specifically allowing or prohibiting surrogacy agreements.

ARIZONA
Surrogacy agreements are void and unenforceable.

ARKANSAS
Intended Mothers are recognized as legal mothers by statute, even though surrogacy agreements are not specifically enforceable by statute.

CALIFORNIA
Surrogacy agreements are valid and enforceable by statute, so long as certain requirements are met.

COLORADO
There is no law (case law or statutory) specifically allowing or prohibiting surrogacy agreements.

CONN.
Case law strongly implies no public policy prohibits surrogacy agreements.

DELAWARE
There is no law (case law or statutory) specifically allowing or prohibiting surrogacy agreements.

DISTRICT OF COLUMBIA
Surrogacy agreements are void and unenforceable. It is a felony to facilitate a compensated surrogacy agreement in the District of Columbia.

FLORIDA
Surrogacy agreements are valid and enforceable by statute, so long as certain requirements are met.

GEORGIA
There is no law (case law or statutory) specifically allowing or prohibiting surrogacy agreements.

HAWAII
There is no law (case law or statutory) specifically allowing or prohibiting surrogacy agreements.

IDAHO
There is no law (case law or statutory) specifically allowing or prohibiting surrogacy agreements.

ILLINOIS
Surrogacy agreements are valid and enforceable by statute, so long as certain requirements are met.

INDIANA
Surrogacy agreements are void and unenforceable.

IOWA
There is no law (case law or statutory) specifically allowing or prohibiting surrogacy agreements.

KANSAS	There is no law (case law or statutory) specifically allowing or prohibiting surrogacy agreements.
KENTUCKY	Surrogacy agreements allowing compensation of the surrogate are invalid.
LOUISIANA	Surrogacy agreements allowing compensation of the surrogate are invalid.
MAINE	Case law implies surrogacy agreements may be enforceable. There is no statute specifically allowing or prohibiting surrogacy agreements.
MARYLAND	Case law strongly implies no public policy prohibits surrogacy agreements.
MASSACHUSETTS	Case law implies surrogacy agreements may be enforceable. There is no statute specifically allowing or prohibiting surrogacy agreements.
MICHIGAN	Surrogacy agreements are void and unenforceable. It is a felony to facilitate a compensated surrogacy agreement in Michigan.
MINNESOTA	There is no law (case law or statutory) specifically allowing or prohibiting surrogacy agreements.
MISSISSIPPI	There is no law (case law or statutory) specifically allowing or prohibiting surrogacy agreements.
MISSOURI	There is no law (case law or statutory) specifically allowing or prohibiting surrogacy agreements.
MONTANA	There is no law (case law or statutory) specifically allowing or prohibiting surrogacy agreements.
NEBRASKA	Surrogacy agreements allowing compensation of the surrogate are invalid.
NEVADA	Surrogacy agreements are valid and enforceable, by statute, so long as certain requirements are met.
NEW HAMPSHIRE	Surrogacy agreements are valid and enforceable, by statute, so long as certain requirements are met.
NEW JERSEY	Case law has ruled that adoption laws govern parentage and custody in surrogacy arrangements, and that a compensated surrogacy arrangement is unenforceable. There is no statute specifically allowing or prohibiting surrogacy agreements.

NEW MEXICO	There is no law (case law or statutory) specifically allowing or prohibiting surrogacy agreements.
NEW YORK	Surrogacy agreements void and unenforceable.
NORTH CAROLINA	There is no law (case law or statutory) specifically allowing or prohibiting surrogacy agreements.
NORTH DAKOTA	Surrogacy agreements void and unenforceable.
OHIO	Case law strongly implies no public policy prohibits surrogacy agreements.
OKLAHOMA	There is no law (case law or statutory) specifically allowing or prohibiting surrogacy agreements.
OREGON	There is no law (case law or statutory) specifically allowing or prohibiting surrogacy agreements.
PENN.	There is no law (case law or statutory) specifically allowing or prohibiting surrogacy agreements.
PUERTO RICO	There is no law (case law or statutory) specifically allowing or prohibiting surrogacy agreements.
RHODE ISLAND	There is no law (case law or statutory) specifically allowing or prohibiting surrogacy agreements.
SOUTH CAROLINA	There is no law (case law or statutory) specifically allowing or prohibiting surrogacy agreements.
SOUTH DAKOTA	There is no law (case law or statutory) specifically allowing or prohibiting surrogacy agreements.
TENNESSEE	The definition of "surrogate mother" in Tennessee's adoption statute implies that a gestational surrogacy contract is valid if the Intended Parents are married. Other than that, there is no law (case law or statutory) specifically allowing or prohibiting surrogacy agreements.
TEXAS	Surrogacy agreements are valid and enforceable, by statute, so long as certain requirements are met. Intended parents must be married.
UTAH	Surrogacy agreements are valid and enforceable, by statute, so long as certain requirements are met.
VERMONT	There is no law (case law or statutory) specifically allowing or prohibiting surrogacy agreements.
VIRGINIA	Surrogacy agreements are valid and enforceable, by statute, so long as certain requirements are met.

WASHINGTON Surrogacy agreements allowing compensation of the surrogate are invalid.

WEST VIRGINIA There is no law (case law or statutory) specifically allowing or prohibiting surrogacy agreements.

WISCONSIN The Wisconsin Supreme Court has found a surrogacy agreement to be enforceable so long as it was in the best interests of the child. There is no statute which applies, allowing or prohibiting surrogacy agreements.

WYOMING There is no law (case law or statutory) specifically allowing or prohibiting surrogacy agreements.

Courtesy of Tim Schlesinger, Paule Camazine & Blumenthal PC